G R E A T
LITERATURE
AND · THE
GOOD · LIFE

G R E A T
LITERATURE
AND · THE
GOOD · LIFE

Sterling W. Sill

Library of Congress Catalog Card No.: 85-080542
ISBN: 0-88290-305-5
Horizon Publishers Catalog & Order No.: 2003

Printed and distributed
in the United States of America by

Horizon
Publishers
& Distributors, Incorporated

50 South 500 West   P.O. Box 490
Bountiful, Utah 84010-0490

Contents

Introduction

One who acquires a new radio or television set, or an automobile, or even a can opener, usually gets with it instructions on how to make the best possible use of the new possession. When one goes into a business building, he usually first looks for the building directory to know how to get where he wants to go.

Even so, it may be helpful to have an introduction or preface to a book to serve as a friendly greeter or forerunner to help make the reader feel more welcome and at home as the introduction points out directions a particular book will take.

Two of the most important aids to successful living are: first, a thorough mastery of a language to think with; second, ideals to nourish our minds and strengthen our success and happiness. Try to imagine what it was like to have lived when the earth was young, when there was no scripture, no printing presses, no great literature.

It has been said that the book is the world's greatest creation. In support of this thesis someone has said, "Books are among life's most precious possessions. They are the most remarkable creation of man. Nothing else that man builds ever lasts. Monuments fall, civilizations perish, but books continue. The perusal of a good book is, as it were, an interview with the noblest men of past ages who have written it."

Charles Kingsley said:

> There is nothing more wonderful than a book. It may be a message to us from the dead, from human souls we never saw who lived perhaps thousands of miles away. And yet these little sheets of paper speak to us, arouse us, teach us, open our hearts, and in turn open their hearts to us like brothers. Without books God is silent, justice dormant, philosophy lame.

John Milton said, "Books are not . . . dead things, but do [contain a certain potency] of life in them . . . as active as that soul whose progeny they are; they preserve as in a vial the purest efficacy . . . of that living intellect that bred them."

There is an ancient legend that tells of a time when the world lost the Bible. Not only did the book itself disappear, but all traces of its influence were taken completely from the earth. Its doctrines had vanished. Its philosophy, its commandments, its history, and its religion were all as completely erased from the records of the world as though they had never existed.

Priceless archives appeared as though vandals had pillaged them, slashing and despoiling the classical works of the world. Art galleries now displayed empty frames. Valuable religious canvases had been taken away, leaving no trace of the thrilling artistry inspired by the Bible.

Much of the finest music in the world was silenced, evaporated as though it had never existed. Mighty oratorios such as *The Messiah*, *The Creation*, and the *Elijah* were out of circulation forever. They had not only been removed from libraries and galleries, but they were also completely expunged from the minds and hearts of men. Beautiful hymns which for ages had expressed the hopes, the fears, the devotions of millions were now silent. Beautiful Christmas carols, Easter anthems, songs of Thanksgiving were no more.

Libraries had been gutted. The writings of Shakespeare, Milton, Tennyson, Carlyle, Longfellow, and countless others were dull and drab since they lacked their former inspiration and beauty. Masterpieces of oratory were without their most potent passages. Law books made little sense because the fundamental principles of right and justice had been eliminated. Great documents of human rights such as the Magna Carta of Great Britain, the Constitution of the United States, the Declaration of Independence were now as sounding brass.

Great values had become jumbled and confused. Precious gifts of the spirit were blurred, cancelled out, and in their place was nothing but blankness.

When the Bible was lost, according to the legend, the Holy Spirit was also snuffed out; in its absence man no longer grew tall of soul, gentle of spirit, courageous of heart, just and honest toward his fellowmen, faithful in life, fearless in death. Life itself had become flat, empty, and purposeless for God, the author of the Bible, had also vanished leaving man no one to worship but himself. Natural laws by which the universe had been governed now had no author, no master. Everything was left to chance, and confusion reigned.

Fortunately this was only a legend. We still have the Bible. The Book of books is still on the shelf where it has always been. The word of God is still available. We can turn to its greatest passages with a moment's notice. How fortunate we are to have this holy book and all that goes with it in our immediate possession. It has given more inspiration to more people than any other book ever printed.

The fate of nations—and everyone in them—hangs on the holy scriptures. Napoleon on St. Helena said:

> The Bible is not merely a book—it is a living power . . . Nowhere as in the Bible can be found such a series of beautiful ideas and admirable maxims which pose before us like the battalions of a celestial army . . . The soul can never go astray while it has this book for its guide.

Even the holy scriptures serve no useful purpose in our lives if we don't know what they say and if we fail to follow their precepts. Some people are mere "Bible Christians" where all the Christianity remains in the Bible and none of it gets into them.

The most brilliant minds in the earth's history have written their most helpful ideas and have left them for us in the world's great literature. But, like the Bible, what good do they do us if we are unfamiliar with them?

The greatest of all literary authorities has said, ". . . seek ye out of the best books words of wisdom; seek learning, even by study and also by faith" (D&C 88:118). When the Lord made this statement, He certainly did not have in mind those books that are filled with violence, crime, sex orgies, and other forms of ungodliness.

When we sing *God Bless America* what kind of an America do we have in mind? Certainly not a drunken America, nor an immoral America, nor a disloyal, ungodly, irresponsible America. Nor do we want an ignorant, uninformed America.

We should be familiar with the great histories, the great biographies. We should be familiar with the great success stories, the great love stories, the great philosophies. It would also be a good idea to memorize potent passages from great poetry and other literary works. Our literature also may give us extra, pleasant hours as well as furnish contrasts and comparisons which may help us to evaluate and direct our own lives.

This little volume is intended to be a kind of sales talk, a recommendation, since there is an important connection for each of us to make between the "Great Literature and The Good Life." Man is a thinking being; what and how we think largely determines what we are and what we will become.

A Famine in the Land

One problem that faces our world is famines that cut down the earth's food supply. God promised to make the nation of ancient Israel the greatest nation on the earth. When He gave the Israelites their promised land, He told them it would be a land flowing with milk and honey, that it would produce abundantly of vines and pomegranates and other good things. The bodies of the people were to be immune from disease.

But, even in Abraham's day, he and his wife were forced to go into Egypt to avoid the risk of starvation. Abraham, his grandson Jacob, and his great-grandsons—who later became the leaders of the Twelve Tribes of Israel—were all forced to take up residence in Egypt because of the scanty food supply in their own chosen land.

Today many parts of the world have been stricken with famine. Many people are suffering from malnutrition. People are starving in places such as India and Africa.

But there is more than one kind of famine. The prophet Amos mentioned a famine which was not a famine for bread nor a thirst for water, but for hearing the word of the Lord (see Amos 8:11-13). There are many people whose spirits are starving; a spiritual food supply is as important as a storehouse of bread.

In Maxwell Anderson's play, *The Masque of Kings*, he has his leading character, Rudolph, say:

> If you'll go stop
> three tradesmen on the street, and ask the three
> what it is they live by, they'll reply at once
> bread, meat and drink, and they'll be certain of it;
> victuals and drink, like the rhyme in Mother Goose
> makes up their diet; nothing will be said
> of faith in things unseen, or following
> the gleam, just bread and meat and a can of wine
> to wash it down. But if you know them well

behind the fish-eyes and the bellies, if
you know them better than they do, each one
burns candles at some altar of his mind
in secret; secret often from himself
each is a priest to some dim mystery
by which he lives. Strip him of that, and bread
and meat and wine won't nourish him.
. . . without his . . . hidden faith
he dies and goes to dust.

We can live on less if we have more to live for. We can live without the great scriptures and other great literature, but not very well. We need a good dose of inspiration occasionally. We need to banish the plagues of famine and ignorance that still afflict many parts of our world.

There is more curative power in books than in bottles. The Lord Himself has said, "It is impossible for a man to be saved in ignorance" (D&C131:6). Neither can anyone be saved in idleness, indecision, or indifference to learning.

The Lord has said, "Blessed are they which do hunger and thirst after righteousness: for they shall be filled" (Matt. 5:6). We might also say, "Blessed are they who do hunger and thirst after wisdom, and culture, and honor, and success, and happiness, for they also shall be satisfied."

What an awful death it would be to die of ignorance, or coarseness, or indifference, or boredom. We must not allow ourselves to starve to death while attending the greatest banquet that life has ever offered to any group of people who have ever lived upon this earth.

Studies in Reading

Reading may be one of the most profitable experiences in anyone's life. This is a rather mysterious process whereby we get ideas, philosophies, enthusiasms, and faith out of the greatest minds and into our own. Anything that is read can be clear profit since there is no obligation to take anything but the best.

The first eight years of my own formal reading experience took place while I was in grammar school. For about an hour each day the teacher conducted a reading class. At the beginning of each new year we were issued one in a series of books entitled *Studies in Reading*. These books were compiled by W. Searson, professor of English at the University of Nebraska, and George E. Martin, president of the State Teachers College at Kearny, Nebraska.

These readers contained great poetry, specially selected prose and bits of wisdom. The readers had thrilling stories of patriotism and other ideas pointing toward good citizenship and the good life. There were passages taken from the Holy Bible, while still others glorified the family and honored God.

We studied Victor Hugo's *Les Miserables*, Patrick Henry's *Call to Arms*, the speech of John Adams favoring the adoption of the Declaration of Independence, Abraham Lincoln's story of *The Soldier's Reprieve* by R. D. S. Robbins, William Cullen Bryant's *Thanatopsis*, James Russell Lowell's *Vision of Sir Launfal*, and Joseph Addison's *Mountain of Miseries*.

Back in those days we memorized a great deal. I can still recite many of those wonderful literary treasures I learned by heart over sixty-five years ago. Later, while I was serving as a teacher, it was my pleasant privilege to direct some of these reading classes; and among my most treasured possessions are copies of the old readers we used in the fifth through eighth grades.

Apparently these books were first published in 1910; and it is a very pleasant experience for me now to think of the "old days" and the inspiring materials that were taught during that period. Naturally the things we learn while we are young and impressionable have an important effect on us for the rest of our lives.

From the preface of one of these books, I have copied this introduction:

> Reading with appreciation is a fine art. It is the purpose of this volume to provide the means whereby the reader may obtain a more intelligent appreciation of some of the most inspiring short poems and selected prose that are to be found in the English language. The poems are selected to cover a wide range of appeal in every good grade and uplifting variety of emotion.
>
> Each subject presented for study has a helpful introduction. Next comes the selection itself. In third place are some suggested questions which may be studied for additional understanding and appreciation. And finally there is a list of references calling attention to other helpful related selections.
>
> The introduction brings the reader's mind into a constructive attitude and provides the atmosphere in which the selection may be most appreciated. The questions at the end afford the student the means of deepening and intensifying that appreciation. Notes are given to make sure that he understands those references that may not at first be clear to him. The titles of other helpful and related material that follow permit one to widen his appreciation into other fields. With such directed effort he can learn to read the selection with genuine appreciation.
>
> He is taught how to study and how to do his homework. And through the class recitation period, he is taught expression and complete familiarity with the best thought and the highest feelings known in our world. This reading activity should bring the student face to face with the fundamental truths and beauty of such selections as *America the Beautiful*, Paul's speech on Mars Hill, the *Chambered Nautilus*, and Joaquin Miller's *Columbus*.

Authors of this literature have already passed away, yet these magnificent volumes are as fresh, as dynamic today as they were when they were first published in 1910. I know of nothing that has been as valuable to me as was this hour a day I spent reading in grammar school.

I have had some powerful experiences with books since that time. I like to imagine that, instead of books, the shelf in my library actually contains a collection of great human beings where I may have the best of each as his service is needed by me.

Associates are often imposed on us, but our reading may be the result of our own choice. Today, instead of spending an hour reading the great literature, the great scriptures, many people read about crime waves, errors in government, bitterness in human relationships. The man who chooses the right books and papers becomes, perhaps unconsciously, more accurate in his thinking, more rooted in his convictions. His mind gains greater strength.

The life and feelings of a young girl who is fascinated by a glowing love story has her attitudes colored and shaped by the page that she reads. If the writing be false, and weak, and foolish, she may become false, and weak, and foolish, too. But if it be true, and tender, and inspiring, then some of this truth, tenderness, and inspiration will grow into her soul to become a part of her very self.

The boy who reads about deeds of manliness, or bravery, or noble daring feels a spirit of emulation grow within him. The seed is planted which will bring forth fruit of heroic endeavor and an exalted life.

About books, Ralph Waldo Emerson said:

> Consider what you have in the smallest well-chosen library—a company of the wisest and wittiest men which can be plucked out of all civilized countries in a thousand years. The men themselves were then hidden and inaccessible. They were solitary, impatient of interruption, and fenced by etiquette. But now they are immortal, and the thought they did not reveal, even to their bosom friends, is here written out in transparent words of light to us, who are strangers of another age.

About this immortality of the mind, Henry Pestalozzi said:

> So when a great man dies
> For years beyond our ken
> The light he leaves behind him lies
> Upon the paths of men.

If we need encouragement, or to be motivated by our faith, we may read from some treasured volume the philosophy of our choice. In his poem, *The Day Is Done*, Henry Wadsworth Longfellow said:

> The day is done, and the darkness
> Falls from the wings of Night,

As a feather is wafted downward
From an eagle in his flight.

I see the lights of the village
Gleam through the rain and the mists,
And a feeling of sadness comes o'er me
That my soul cannot resist:

The feeling of sadness and longing
That is not akin to pain,
And resembles sorrow only
As the mist resembles the rain.

Come, read to me some poem,
Some simple and heartfelt lay,
That shall soothe this restless feeling,
And banish the thoughts of day.

Not from the grand old masters,
Not from the bards sublime,
Whose distant footsteps echo
Through the corridors of Time.

For, like strains of martial music,
Their mighty thoughts suggest
Life's endless toil and endeavor;
And to-night I long for rest.

Read from some humbler poet,
Whose songs gushed from his heart,
As showers from the clouds of summer,
Or tears from the eyelids start;

Who, through long days of labor,
And nights devoid of ease,
Still heard in his soul the music
Of wonderful melodies.

Such songs have power to quiet
The restless pulse of care,
And come like the benediction
That follows after prayer.

> Then read from the treasured volume
> The poem of thy choice,
> And lend to the rhyme of the poet
> The beauty of thy voice.
>
> And the night shall be filled with music,
> And the cares, that infest the day,
> Shall fold their tents, like the Arabs,
> And as silently steal away.

We not only lend to the rhyme of the poet the beauty of our own voice, but we also let the imagination of our own interest fill the night with music, the day with success.

Horatio Alger wrote some two hundred thirty-five books, filled with the "rags to riches" success stories which may actually draw the reader upward. We have stories of industry where the labor thrust may be transferred to our own personalities. We have human interest stories in every field along with stories of high motivation. There are stories of patriotism, hero stories, stories of success that need to be continually stamped into our minds.

James Montgomery might add to our philosophy of patriotism when he says:

> There is a land, of every land the pride,
> Beloved by Heaven o'er all the world beside;
> Where brighter suns dispense serener light,
> And milder moons imparadise the night;
> A land of beauty, virtue, valor, truth,
> Time-tutored age, and love-exalted youth.
> Where shall that land, that spot of earth be found?
> Art thou a man? a patriot? look around!
> Oh! thou shalt find, howe'er thy footsteps roam,
> That land thy country, and that spot thy home.

One of the most regrettable problems of our age is that we are forgetting how to read. When people began to buy clocks and watches, they lost the ability to tell time by the sun. When an arm is tied up in a sling, the muscle may begin to deteriorate. When we support ourselves with crutches, we risk losing the power in our legs. And those who become entirely dependent on television and radio for their information may lose the finest values in their lives.

We put the capstone on this chapter, "Studies in Reading," with a fervent prayer that above almost every other thing, God will bless us that we may learn to read well by reading well. And this is also the place where we might confer our richest blessings upon ourselves.

3

Literature—Noblest of the Professions

Man is a thinking being. Thoughts not only rule the world, but they determine what our individual lives will someday be. Victor Hugo added to this philosophy when he said, "The greatest power in the world is an idea whose time has come." And an idea's time comes when we are able to get a harness on it so that it can do its assigned work of producing greatness in our lives.

Abraham Lincoln once expressed the need of each person when he said: "What I want to know is in books, and my best friend is the one who will get me a book I haven't read." Abraham Lincoln lived in the days when books were scarce, and the money which might make available the ideas from libraries was even scarcer.

Lincoln quoted scriptures throughout his life to make his points. He may help us understand what Edgar Allen Poe meant when he said that literature is the noblest of the professions.

Literature is the profession that has to do with building character, personality, religion, success, and happiness in other people. The Lord Himself must have had a very high opinion of the importance of literature for He was the greatest author and the greatest student of good literature.

The wise man, Solomon, said: "Wisdom is the principal thing; therefore get wisdom: and with all thy getting get understanding" (Prov. 4:7). Yet the wise statements made by him and other important men are not always followed by us.

Thomas A. Edison commented on one of man's basic weaknesses when he said: "There is almost no limit to which a man will not go to avoid thinking." Yet Solomon said: "As a man thinketh in his heart, so is he." Certainly if we are what we think, and if we don't think, we might expect to have problems, one of which would be mental and spiritual malnutrition and stagnation.

4

I Got a Glory

Archibald Rutledge wrote a delightful book entitled *My Colonel and His Lady* in which he related an interesting experience he had as a lad on the Santee River in central South Carolina. This particular incident had to do with an old Negro riverboat captain who piloted the ferry boat, *Foam*. The boat was dirty, odorous, and badly kept.

But one day, when Dr. Rutledge went down to the river, he found the *Foam* completely transformed. It was clean from stem to stern. It fairly gleamed and glistened in the sunlight. The boat's brass had been polished until it shined like many mirrors. The bilge water was gone from behind the seats, and the deck had been scoured to the raw wood. No less miraculous was the transformation in the Negro captain himself. He was shining and immaculate. His face beamed, his eyes sparkled. He sat behind the *Foam's* wheel with an open Bible in his lap.

When Dr. Rutledge asked him the reason for this wonderful transformation, he gave a formula for living which each of us ought to stamp deep into our own brain cells. He said, "I got a glory." Great ideas had gotten into the captain's brain, and great applications had gotten into his bloodstream. These had made him a different man. He now had the glory of a lighted mind, the glory of a quickened personality. He had the glory of a grand ambition.

The transformation so apparent in the riverboat was only a manifestation of a far more important transformation in the captain himself. His work had not changed; he was still a riverboat captain. But he was now the best riverboat captain on the Santee. Henceforth, whatever he did would indicate this change. His life's work would indicate his life's glory.

But the story of the Negro riverboat captain is the story of every man, for every man manifests his greatness in his work. If he isn't great in what he does, he isn't great. "No man can have a high and noble character while engaged in petty or mean employment, for whatever the pursuits of men are their characters will be similar." You can't have a glory while you have bilge water under your seats, or a sour attitude about life, or a chronic, disabling case of battle fatigue.

This qualification of glory is an attribute of God Himself, as Julia Ward Howe said in her poem:

> In the beauty of the lilies Christ was born across the sea,
> With a glory in His bosom that transfigures you and me;
> As He died to make men holy, let us die to make men free,
>   While God is marching on.

When Moses visited with God on the top of Mt. Sinai, the glory of God rested upon Moses so that he could endure God's presence. Then when Moses went down to communicate with his own people, he had to put a covering over his own face so that the people could endure his presence.

This term "glory" may mean different things to different people under different circumstances. The dictionary defines glory as "the condition of highest achievement, the highest degree of pleasure, satisfaction, splendor, magnificence, radiance." A glory is represented in art by a halo of light over one's head. But in our spirituality, and in our lives, it isn't just over our heads—it is in our heads and in our hearts and in our habits and shines forth through our eyes.

We should not wait until the next world to think about getting a glory. If we want to be great souls in heaven, we had better practice being great souls here. If we are going to be better later on, we should start being better now. We may not know all about the glory of the next world, but we can know and do know quite a lot about a glory in this world. The glory that the old captain had is the kind that gets things done; it shines forth from your heart and gets into your handshake. Above almost everything else, we need to learn how to live with a glory.

A glory can't be kept a secret. It makes your life different. It helps you to be "born again." As the condition of the *Foam* was merely a visible expression of the condition of the captain, just so, everything we have and everything we are, are merely outward signs of what is inside us.

We cannot improve our circumstances unless we first improve ourselves. Success cannot be found in San Francisco, or New York, or Cincinnati until it is first found inside of us. That is where most of the really important things are found. It doesn't matter very much what is behind us or what is before us; the thing that is important is what is inside of us.

The increased strength that always comes from the development of inner qualities in a great man may have been what Jesus referred to when He said, ". . . I have meat to eat that ye know not of" (John 4:32). But anyone who has a glory feeds on a vitalizing diet which makes the hardest tasks easy.

Indians told Columbus that they were growing an herb that took away fatigue. But there are many things that will take away fatigue. One is a vigorous, positive attitude of mind. Another is a vital purity of purpose when fatigue is lost and an increase of strength and enthusiasm is gained. No one ever gets tired while he is winning. No one ever loses interest while he is ahead.

We must learn to work harder and more effectively if we want to get ahead. We get battle fatigue only when the burden is too unwieldy for that which animates it. The answer is not a smaller objective; it is a greater power. We need to learn how to live under a higher voltage.

Solomon said that there is a time to live and a time to die. Then he pointed out that there are a few things we should do in between. One of them is to clean up the ferry boats of our success and make them sparkle with accomplishment. There is no excellence without labor. That Aladdin's palace was built by a magic genie for a lazy occupant is only a fairy tale. We should not count too much on such lazy daydreams or on easy miracles to bring us a glory.

Dr. Alan Stockdale has pointed out that God left the world unfinished for man to work his skill upon. He left electricity still in the clouds, oil still in the earth. He left rivers unbridged, forests unfelled, cities unbuilt. God gave to man the challenge of raw materials, not the ease of finished things. He left pictures unpainted, music unsung, problems unsolved that man might know the joys and glories of creation. God supplies the quarries, but He carves the statues and builds the cathedrals only by the hand of man.

God has also left the world of men unfinished. The creation of man was not something that was completed and done within the Garden of Eden six thousand years ago. The creation of man is still going on, and we are the creators. That is, we are presently generating the enthusiasm and the faith and the understanding and the industry that will determine the quality of our lives.

The greatest blessings, as well as the greatest powers of our lives, come disguised in work clothes demanding of us, like the stern Roman soldier, that we travel with him for that one hard mile. The ancient law gave the Roman the right to compel anyone to carry his soldier burdens for one mile. But Jesus didn't stop there. He said, ". . . whosoever shall compel thee to go a mile, go with him twain" (Matt. 5:41). Doing more than is expected is one of the best ways to get a glory.

A glory takes compulsion out of our lives and fills our hearts with cheer. It releases in us an unheard of strength, an undreamed of satisfaction. A glory takes the frown from our face, the weariness from the body and makes the second mile a pleasure trip. A glory makes one wish there were more hours in the day.

A glory translates duty into pleasure. It also enables us to say, "I have meat to eat that ye know not of." Scrubbing the decks of a riverboat may be drudgery to some, but there is no drudgery when you've got a glory. To go a mile by compulsion may be so wearisome and hateful as to break down our strength, but to go two miles on our own power is a lot of fun when we've got a glory.

To fail to get a glory is to fail to get sufficient enthusiasm to make our part of the work of the world an interesting, fascinating game. It is an exciting thing to live with a glory. A glory makes everything glorious.

> The sun is up and it is day
> The bird is on the wing
> The ant, its labor has begun
> And the woods with music ring.

When we get a glory it doesn't matter whether the weather is cold or hot, whether conditions are good or bad. Obstacles and difficulties become of little consequence, for then, in any circumstance, we are able to say with the old riverboat captain, "I got a glory!"

5

Hamlet

In a literary survey compiled by Daniel Starck, Shakespeare's *Hamlet* was voted the greatest book ever written, second only to the Bible. The Holy Bible was given first place, as it should have been because we realize that the Bible was written by men who were speaking directly for God.

Many of the greatest literary works are filled with references and other allusions to the scriptures. The writings of Shakespeare, for example, contain some five hundred references to the Bible.

Excluding those men who spoke directly for God, most people probably think of Shakespeare as being the greatest writer who ever lived. Shakespeare looked with keen insight into human lives. He wrote thirty-seven plays staffed with a thousand characters, each personifying a special personality trait. The Bard of Avon said that his purpose in writing was to hold a mirror up to life to show virtue her own image and scorn her own likeness.

In *Julius Caesar*, Shakespeare has his character Cassius say:

> I your [looking] glass
> Will [be and will] modestly discover to yourself
> [qualities] of yourself which you yet know not of.
> (*Julius Caesar*, Act I, sc. ii)

In his plays we can see a reflection of our own lives as we watch his players act and react upon each other. If *Hamlet* is to be considered the greatest of all Shakespeare's works, it may be helpful to know why. A very brief story of Hamlet follows:

Hamlet, the king of Denmark, was sleeping in his garden when his brother, Claudius, poured a quick-acting poison into his ear that went coursing through his blood like quicksilver and caused his death. It was reported to the people that the king had been bitten by a serpent. In less than two months Claudius married Hamlet's queen, ascended the throne, and took over the rule and resources of Denmark.

Hamlet's son, whose name was also Hamlet, had a suspicion that something was wrong. He said, "Something is rotten in the state of Denmark" (*Hamlet*, Act I, sc. iv).

While the young prince was trying to find out what it was, he learned that the late king's ghost had been seen in the dead of night, stalking the gloomy battlements of the castle. In a terrifying encounter, Hamlet learned from the specter that his father had been murdered by Claudius.

The young prince committed himself to revenging his father's death. The rest of the play has to do with him carrying out this oath. In the process, all of the principals in the play lose their lives.

Shakespeare was a great author for many reasons. For one, he understood human nature. He said: "Conceit in weakest bodies strongest works" (*Hamlet*, Act III, sc. iv). He knew how to appeal to human interest. Certainly he was not dull. He was great for the impetus he gave to self-improvement. He said, "Assume a virtue, if you have it not" (*Hamlet*, Act III, sc. iv).

He dealt with the important subjects of life, and of death, and of success. He knew the place of good and evil in human lives. He was an architect of speech. He understood how to exalt and polish the most simple of expressions. He was an artist in using language beautifully and effectively. He was also a wise philosopher. Consider:

. . . for to the noble mind
Rich gifts wax poor when givers prove unkind.
(*Hamlet*, Act III, sc. i)

Again,

Neither a borrower nor a lender be:
For loan oft loses both itself and friend,
And borrowing dulls the edge of husbandry.
(*Hamlet*, Act I, sc. iii)

Again,

This above all: to thine own self be true,
And it must follow, as the night the day,
Thou canst not then be false to any man.
(*Hamlet*, Act I, sc. iii)

Young Hamlet loved his father, the king, very much. He said of him:

[Here] was a man: take him for all in all,
[I think] I shall not look upon his like again.
(*Hamlet*, Act I, sc. ii)

He said:

What a piece of work is . . . man! how noble in reason! how infinite in faculty! in form and moving how express and admirable! in action how like an angel! in apprehension how like a god! the beauty of the world! the paragon of animals! (*Hamlet*, Act II, sc. ii)

Shakespeare also made powerful statements centered in human weakness. Those human frailties in young Hamlet's weak-willed mother helped touch the young prince with a case of melancholia to the point where he contemplated suicide. He was restrained by fear of the penalty which God has attached to taking one's own life. In his despondency he said,

O, that this too too solid flesh would melt
Thaw and resolve itself into a dew!
Or that the Everlasting had not fix'd
His canon 'gainst self-slaughter! O God! God!
How weary, stale, flat and unprofitable
Seem to me all the uses of this world!
. . . 'tis [like] an unweeded garden,
That grows to seed; things rank and gross in nature
Possess it merely.
(*Hamlet*, Act I, sc. ii)

Young Hamlet's doubt that life was worthwhile prompted this famous soliloquy:

To be, or not to be: that is the question:
Whether 'tis nobler in the mind to suffer
The slings and arrows of outrageous fortune,
Or to take [up] arms against a sea of troubles,
And by opposing end them. To die: to sleep;
No more; and by a sleep to say we end
The heart-ache, and the thousand natural shocks
That flesh is heir to, 'tis a consummation

Devoutly to be wish'd. To die, to sleep;
To sleep: perchance to dream: ay, there's the rub;
For in that sleep of death what dreams may come,
When we have shuffled off this mortal coil,
Must give us pause: there's the respect
That makes calamity of so long life;
For who would bear the whips and scorns of time,
The oppressor's wrong, the proud man's contumely,
The pangs of despised love, the law's delay,
The insolence of office, and the spurns
That patient merit of the unworthy takes,
When he himself might his quietus make
With a bare bodkin? who would fardels bear,
To grunt and sweat under a weary life,
But that the dread of something after death,
The undiscover'd country from whose bourn
No traveller returns, puzzles the will,
And makes us rather bear those ills we have
Than fly to others that we know not of?
Thus conscience does make cowards of us all.
(*Hamlet*, Act III, sc. i)

Hamlet had died in his sleep without having a chance to repent.
Therefore, according to a particular theology, his soul was sent to hell.
In the midnight rendezvous with his son, his ghost touches our interest
as he describes this situation. He said:

[Hamlet] I am thy father's spirit;
Doom'd for a certain term to walk the night,
And for the day confined to fast in fires,
Till the foul crimes done in my days of nature
Are burnt and purged away. But that I am forbid
To tell the secrets of my prison-house,
I would a tale unfold whose lightest word
Would harrow up thy soul, freeze thy young blood,
Make thy two eyes, like stars, start from their spheres,
Thy knotted and combined locks to part
And each particular hair to stand on end,
Like quills upon the fretful porpentine:
But this eternal blazon must not be
To ears of flesh and blood.

. . . Now, Hamlet, hear:
'Tis given out that, sleeping in my orchard,
A serpent stung me; . . .
but know, thou noble youth,
The serpent that did sting thy father's life
Now wears his crown.
. . . List, list, O, list!
If thou didst ever thy dear father love—
. . . Revenge his foul and most unnatural murder.
(*Hamlet*, Act I, sc. v)

As the spirit scented the approach of morning air and knew he
must depart, he bade a quick farewell to his son by saying, "Hamlet,
adieu, remember me." Then, under the stress of a most determined
resolve, the son replied:

. . . Remember thee!
Ay, thou poor ghost, while memory holds a seat
In this distracted globe. Remember thee!
Yea, from the table of my memory
I'll wipe away all trivial fond records,
All saws of books, all forms, all pressures past,
That youth and observation copied there;
And thy commandment all alone shall live
Within the book and volume of my brain,
Unmix'd with baser matter . . .
(*Hamlet*, Act I, sc. v)

But first Hamlet decided he needed more proof of his uncle's guilt.
He reasoned that, inasmuch as the devil had the power to assume a
pleasing shape, the spirit he had seen may have been Satan trying to
entice him to commit a murder in order to damn him. He said:

. . . yea . . . Out of my weakness and my melancholy,
[Satan, who) is very potent with such spirits,
[May be] abus[ing] me to damn me."
(*Hamlet*, Act II, sc. ii)

A group of traveling players were then in the castle. Hamlet
arranged for them to enact a similar murder play before his uncle
while he watched his uncle's face for the tell-tale indication of his guilt.
He said:

. . . I have heard
That guilty creatures, sitting at a play,
Have by the very cunning of the scene
Been struck so to the soul that presently
They have proclaim'd their malefactions;
For murder, though it have no tongue, will speak
With most miraculous organ. I'll have these players
Play something like the murder of my father
Before mine uncle: I'll observe his looks;
I'll tent him to the quick: if he but blench,
I know my course . . .
(*Hamlet*, Act II, sc. ii)

He said:

. . . The play's the thing
Wherein I'll catch the conscience of the king.
(*Hamlet*, Act II, sc. ii)

When the players reached the murder scene, the panic-stricken king arose from his seat, hastily broke up the performance and left the room. Hamlet was then convinced of his uncle's guilt, and he looked for an opportunity to avenge his father's death.

Hamlet's chance soon came to kill his uncle when, unbeknown to Claudius, Hamlet entered his room. But he found Claudius on his knees praying aloud. Claudius prayed:

O, my offence is rank, it smells to heaven;
It hath the primal eldest curse upon 't,
A brother's murder. Pray can I not,
Though inclination be as sharp as will:
My stronger guilt defeats my strong intent,
. . . What if this cursed hand
Were thicker than itself with brother's blood,
Is there not rain enough in the sweet heavens
To wash it white as snow?
. . . Then I'll look up;
My fault is past. But O, what form of prayer
Can serve my turn? 'Forgive me my foul murder?'
That cannot be, since I am still possess'd
Of those effects for which I did the murder,

My crown, mine own ambition and my queen.
May one be pardon'd and retain the offence?
(*Hamlet*, Act III, sc. iii)

Hamlet felt that if he killed Claudius while he was praying, the latter's soul would then be clean and would go to heaven, thus thwarting his own revenge. He said:

A villain kills my father; and for that,
I, his sole son, do this same villain send
To heaven.

Therefore, he left the room to await a more appropriate time. However, the king was not satisfied that his prayer was of much help to him. Arising from his prayer he said:

My words fly up, my thoughts remain below:
Words without thoughts never to heaven go.

Finally Hamlet killed the king with a poisoned sword point that the king had prepared for the prince, and the tragedy of Hamlet came to an end.

In pointing out a comparison, Shakespeare said:

All the world's a stage,
And all the men and women merely players:
. . . [each] in his time plays many parts.
(*As You Like It*, Act II, sc. vii)

May each of us play our own part well. May each of our lives have the most satisfactory and happy ending.

6

Dante and Beatrice

We have many important categories in our literature. Many people have been helped by reading hero and success stories. Occasionally we should all reread and reabsorb the great love stories. One of the most famous of these is that of Dante and Beatrice.

Durante Alighieri, whom we know as Dante, was born in Florence, Italy, in the year 1265. He emerged out of that long night of darkness called the Middle Ages to become the father of modern literature. Dante was supreme in his field. He was an artist with words. He was an architect of thought. He knew the value of symbols. His language was filled with beautiful imagery and stimulating ideas. Longfellow said of him, "Ne'er walked the earth a greater man than he."

Dante's outstanding work was *The Divine Comedy*. In those days, a comedy was not something that was funny—it was something that had a happy ending. A more understandable title of this literary work for our day would be *The Divine Story*, or *The Divine Experience*.

Thomas Carlyle said that *The Divine Comedy*, in his opinion, was the most remarkable book ever written. It was based on scriptural references to eternal punishment. To these scriptural texts Dante added generously from his own scholarly imagination.

The Divine Comedy is divided into three parts. Part one is called "The Inferno." It tells of an imaginary trip Dante made through hell. Dante had been a great admirer of the Roman epic poet, Virgil, who had lived some thirteen hundred years previously. As Dante began his unusual journey in his book, the spirit of Virgil offered to guide him and to explain to him what they saw.

In Dante's story, hell was a place where departed spirits who were forever lost were consigned. These were they whose lives were so warped, twisted, and perverted that there was no hope for their salvation. Through them, Dante shows us the eternal sequel of our lives. He pictures the distorted features of the damned. He shows the intensity of their suffering with a vigor of imagination that may never have been surpassed.

With him we ponder the inscription over the gate of his hell. It said:

> Through me you pass into [a world] of woe;
> Through me you pass into eternal pain;
> . . . Through me [you join the souls forever lost];
> . . . All hope abandon, ye who enter here.

Dante journeyed next through the second kingdom which he called "Purgatory." Here the scenes of suffering were less intense. Dante showed purgatory as God's place of purification. Here certain spirits who had not sinned unto death were cleansed through their own suffering and education.

When sufficient reformation had been made, these spirits were accounted worthy to ascend into heaven. The Bible refers to this place as the place where Jesus preached to the "spirits in prison" who had been disobedient in the days of Noah some 25 centuries earlier. (See 1 Peter 3:19-20.)

Dante believed that it was his mission to show hell to men, and probably there is no more important mission. The Bible speaks of hell as much as it does of heaven. It has been said that there are a thousand people who believe in heaven for every one who believes in hell. But if there is a heaven, there has to be a hell.

Dante pictures hell as a series of circles or elevations. The top levels are inhabited by those spirits who have sinned least. Then, as the descent from one layer to another into the depths of hell continues, the corruption and consequent sufferings increase. Dante tried to picture the worst conceivable suffering of which his mind was capable.

But even at best, the human imagination is limited. It is difficult even to imagine a toothache that hurts as much as the real thing. We do not know how intense either mental or physical suffering can be. We know that it can be severe enough to send one insane. And Dante pictures many of hell's inmates as afflicted with eternal madness because a measure of incurable grief had unhinged their minds.

One of hell's spirits said to Dante, "We beg that if ever you escape from these dark places to look again upon the stars of heaven, see that ye speak of us to other men." And then, in attempting to discharge that obligation, Dante said, "Reader, as God may grant you reason, gather wisdom from reading this and then take counsel with yourself."

The happy ending finally came when Dante went to "Paradise" to conclude his journey, the place where the righteous live forever with God. Dante tried to have us feel the joys of the righteous in heaven and the passion of that great eternal love that helps us get there.

While Dante's love lived largely in the realm of illusion, yet it might effectively represent an eternal affection. Dante's love is the love of a poet. He was a "Pygmalion" who loved his own creation. His love was also a lost love; yet it is often only those things we lose that we really keep.

One-sided loves like that of Dante exist everywhere; the beloved may be as unaware of the love it inspires as the star is of the astronomer who discovers it. Yet even this lost, one-sided love is capable of generating great power in our lives. Dante first saw the lady of his affections when he was nine years old and she was not quite nine. Her name was Beatrice Portinari.

Dante's father was a lawyer. The father of Beatrice was his wealthy client. On this occasion, the senior Dante had taken his son to a lawn party and open house at the surburban Portinari home. As the Dante father and son strolled beneath the trees and were served refreshments by the servants, Dante caught a passing glimpse of Beatrice. They did not speak. He saw her only for an instant amid the dim lights of the flaming garden torches. But upon his youthful mind was impressed a vision of beauty and loveliness that he would carry to his grave.

About this meeting Dante said, "Her dress was of the most noble color, a subdued and goodly crimson, girdled and adorned in such a way as best suited her tender age. At that moment, I say most truly that the spirit of life, which has its dwelling in the most secret chamber of my heart, began to tremble so violently that the least pulses of my body shook therewith; and in trembling it said these words: 'Here is a deity stronger than I, whose coming shall rule over me.' "

Nine more years were to elapse before Dante was ever to speak to Beatrice, though he infers that he caught glimpses of her at church. (It would be difficult for anyone to tell where his love ended and his religion began.)

Dante left Florence for a time, but after several years absence, he returned to meet Beatrice face to face. She was eighteen; and this was the first, the last, the only time they ever met.

She was walking with two women friends, one on either side. She was clothed in pure white. To Dante she looked like an angel of light. Suddenly she stood immediately before him, tall, graceful, intellectual, and smiling. Her eyes looked into his with a sparkle of recognition. The earth seemed to swirl under Dante's feet.

He uncovered his head and was about to sink to his knees, but she sustained him by holding out her hand for him to touch. Then, in greeting she said, "We have missed you from the church and from our streets. You look well, gentle sir. Welcome back to Florence. Good évening." The three women moved on. Dante tried to move but he could not. As he followed her with his eyes, she looked back and smiled.

That day Dante's life began anew; that unexpected meeting, the salutation, the smile wrote themselves into his life forever. The great difference in their social station was no barrier to Dante's love. For the rest of his life he wrote poems to Beatrice. He sang her praises and told of her art and intelligence.

Other affairs again took Dante away from Florence. When Beatrice died in the twenty-fifth year of her life, Dante wrote, "The Lord God of Justice called my most gracious lady to Himself." In her death, Dante was wedded to her memory. He calls her "the bride" of his soul. He said, "Heaven had need of her; she belonged not here, and so God took her to Himself." But Dante was sure that Beatrice would live again in all her loveliness, and he felt that he would see her again in heaven.

As he day-dreamed about her, he agitated his passion. He became more and more devoted to her as the supreme idol of his life. As he thought of her, he thought of Paradise. He felt that she would meet him at the gate and guide him through heaven. As he thought of her, and of heaven and hell, he conceived the idea for *The Divine Comedy*.

This long journey was a magnificent experience with a most happy ending. As Dante and Virgil finally came to the outer borders of the second kingdom, a vast sheet of eternal flame barred their way. Beyond this point Virgil was not permitted to go. Then he said to Dante, "Between Beatrice and thee there is but this wall." This was the moment toward which Dante had been working. He was now face to face with what was, to him, the most glorious of all possibilities.

Immediately he plunged into the very heart of the fire; when we see him next, he is in Paradise. There he beholds his idol, Beatrice, surrounded by a scene of surpassing beauty and magnificence. Heaven is inhabited by an inconceivably glorious company, but none were more beautiful than Beatrice. The eyes of the poet could not sustain the splendor of the view.

As the sublime Beatrice smiled radiantly upon him, she turned Dante and herself toward Him who is the source of all life and light. And thus is realized the happiest of all the "happy endings." Thus also ends the divine trilogy, the noblest literary effort of the Middle Ages.

Even though Dante's supreme love was beyond his reach, yet in his mind its power took him to heaven. The love of Simon Peter for Jesus also led Peter to heaven. Such is the power of a noble ideal. When we love beauty, righteousness, courage, and devotion to God, the noble ideal materializes in our lives and lifts us above the things of this world. A great lover, like a great artist, may sometimes exaggerate his passion. But a far worse danger comes when love's power is too much reduced.

It has been said that the greatest enemy of success is caution. Certainly there is at least one caution that is on the verge of cowardice. It results in halfway measures and casual creeds that lack the power of magnificent accomplishment. Dante devoted the fullest powers of his soul to immortalizing Beatrice; his love for her gave him nobler courage and more powerful incentives.

In the intensity, endurance, and power of this love, Dante probably stands unrivaled. We need more distinctive experiences that will lead us to happier endings. Even the recollections of the great loves of others may sometimes furnish the sparks that will kindle flames of good in us.

The Holy Scriptures say "God is love." The strongest word in our language is love. The strongest passion in our hearts is that potential love of God, righteousness, and success that He has planted there. If our own great experiences are sufficiently developed in us, they may draw us upward to our eternal glory with God Himself guiding our journey.

7

Grace Before Greatness

I once read an article written by the talented American contralto, Marian Anderson. She told of the many personal frustrations and failures she had faced in the beginning of her career. Many obstacles in the way of her success had to be overcome. Miss Anderson's life may serve as an example of problems and discouragements which could fill many unwritten pages in everyone's life. Each of us have some crosses to bear and some miseries to contend with.

Next to God, Marian Anderson credited her success to the evangelical faith and untiring courage of her school-teaching, Bible-reading, widowed mother. Mrs. Anderson tried to encourage Marian to make her own decisions but, because of her problems and hurts, Marian had lost all hope. However, the mother continued to believe in her daughter and kept prodding her as best she could. She suggested that Marian pray her way back into that life-giving, Christ-serving career of music that she, herself, along with many of her friends, believed was the right life for her.

For a long time, Marian brooded much more than she prayed. But her mother's counsel to seek God's help began to take root in her heart. She said, "The longer one lives, the better one realizes that there is no particular endeavor that you can do alone. To accomplish any task, to use one's voice as I do, or even to walk out onto the stage to perform, is not all of one's own doing." Then she added, "I have come to realize that God is a large part of every success, and I recognize that the 'I' part is a very small one."

Marian cherished the quotation from Moses that says: "The eternal God is thy refuge, and underneath are the everlasting arms" (Deut. 33:27). Miss Anderson had many problems, but she said: "Gradually my grief was sufficiently released that I began to pray. In those tearful hours, I realized that there are times when even the most self-sufficient cannot find enough strength to stand alone. Slowly I came out of my despair. My mind began to clear. My self-pity left me. I quit blaming others for my failure."

Then Marian made up her mind to sing; and in a burst of exuberance, she said to her mother: "I want to study again. I want to be the best. I want to be loved by everyone and be perfect in everything." Subsequently Marian sang before kings and presidents; she received great honors.

When the publishers of Miss Anderson's article entitled it, "Grace Before Greatness," they gave us an important suggestion for our own success. After Marian had developed the grace, the greatness was not long in coming. In trying to follow this idea of grace, we discover some eighteen different meanings listed in the dictionary, all of them good ones.

The word grace may mean "a favor of kindness," or an "exhibition of good will." It may mean "to be beloved and agreeable." We speak frankly of getting into someone's "good graces." A grace may also be "a prayer in which a blessing is asked for, or a thanks is returned." A grace may be "a disposition to show mercy or give clemency."

We speak of God's grace. He grants us many benefits that we cannot provide for ourselves. This word may describe an attitude of God, but it is probably intended primarily for us. We need grace for every situation. As Shakespeare once said: "When our grace we have forgot, then nothing goes right."

Dictionary definition No. 9 says that grace is attractiveness, or charm. This aesthetic value can be shown in suppleness, ease, spontaneity, and tactful harmony. It is an easy and natural elegance as applied to persons, manners, seemliness, and comeliness. One may be graceful in body, but there is also an important mental grace, an inspiring spiritual grace, and a grace of sincere and gentle thankfulness.

The distinctive Roman statesman, Cicero, once said, "Gratitude is the mother of virtues." It is interesting that almost all the virtues that tend to make our lives worthwhile are born of gratitude.

Miss Anderson pointed out that no one has enough strength to stand alone. Even our earth itself is not an independent earth. At this very instant God is sending us billions of tons of energy and light and warmth from the sun. If the sun's rays were turned off for just a few hours, no life could survive upon this earth. Yet these life-giving, vitamin-filled, heat-packed rays come to us across some ninety-three million miles of dark, dead, empty space that is unbelievably cold. Only when these rays hit our stmosphere do they release their treasures of light and warmth and strength.

It has been estimated that 95 percent of the factors involved in producing our Thanksgiving dinner are provided by God as a free gift, and only 5 percent come from our own efforts. God provides the atmosphere, the rain, the sunshine, the topsoil, and all of the individual elements from which every variety of food is made. Getting our daily bread merely requires that we plant the seed and care for the crop.

God not only made our food possible, He also made it nourishing and pleasant. Thanksgiving is a day of feasting but not on bread alone. Our spirits should also be fed, and we should get God's graciousness into our souls.

John D. Rockefeller, the world's first billionaire, had a severe stomach disease. It was once reported that he offered to give half of his wealth to his chauffeur if he would trade stomachs with him. But who would trade his health for a billion dollars? We should be thankful that God has given us ourselves. After all, we are our own most priceless possession.

At Christmas time an old Dutchman made up a rhyme in which he said:

> When Christmas comes already yet,
> With presents large and presents sweet;
> The things I like to find in my stockings best
> By Jimminy, are my feet.

A little girl once asked: "Why can't we have Christmas every day?" We might echo her question to ask: "Why not be thankful every day? Why not really feel a prayer of grace and a prayer of gratitude for 'God's favor of kindness' every day?" But we are not limited to a grace before eating. We can also have a grace before reading, and a grace before working, and a grace before thinking, and a grace before serving our fellowmen. It has been said that "the service we give is the rent we pay for the space we occupy."

A story has been told about a boat sinking somewhere off the Pacific Northwest coast during a violent storm. A crowd had gathered to watch the battered vessel being pounded to pieces on the rocks offshore. Some sturdy men launched a lifeboat and pulled frantically at the oars to reach the ship in time to rescue the seamen who clung to their fast-disintegrating vessel.

As the small lifeboat came struggling back to shore, someone cried out, "Did you save them?"

"All but one," came the answer through the storm. "There was one we couldn't reach."

A young man stepped forth from the group and called, "Who will come with me to get the other man?" His mother, gray-haired and obviously frantic, called out, "Oh Jim, please don't go! Please don't risk your life. You are all that I have left."

Onlookers knew that this boy's father had drowned at sea, and years ago his brother Bill had sailed away and had never been heard from since. But the boy replied, "Mother, someone has to go." A few others joined him, and together they launched their boat and pulled for the wreck, while those on shore anxiously waited.

Finally the boat was seen to pull away from the wreck and head again for the shore. The crowd watched as the small, frail craft was beaten by the waves. At every plunge of the boat it looked as if it would be crushed like an eggshell. There was silence on the shore as the watchers prayed. For an hour the desperate struggle continued, until the lifeboat was near enough to hail. Then someone shouted, "Did you get the other man?"

In a high, clear, triumphant shout above the roar of the surf came the young man's voice saying, "Yes! And tell my mother that the man we rescued was Bill!"

What a privilege it is that we may serve God and each other. As we feel and express our appreciation *to* God and *for* God, we become more like him. As we recount our blessings, we not only increase them, but we start a whole new brood of virtues operating in our lives.

Suppose we believed, as some claim, that the One who created the sun and each day sends us light, vitality, and inspiration, was no longer on the job; and that our world—and all of the other heavenly bodies—were now in the hands of chance. How long would your automobile stay on the road if you took your hands off the steering wheel? If it takes constant steering to keep an automobile going in a straight line, what about keeping a few billion constellations operating successfully, all going at different speeds and in different directions.

Each year the earth completes a 595-million-mile orbit around the sun. In the year that I was born, it took the earth 365 days,

5 hours, 48 minutes and 45.51 seconds to complete the orbit; in 1985, the earth made this same journey in exactly the same time. During that long period the time of orbit has not gained or lost one second in traveling this tremendous distance. I must give myself more leeway than that just to get out of bed in the morning.

Dictionary definition No. 13 says that grace is "an unmerited divine favor"; a free gift given by God for the regeneration and sanctification of man. But God's grace operates in numberless ways for the material and spiritual well-being of every human being.

In addition to being thankful *to* God and *for* God, we should also be thankful for our families. We should be thankful for our homes and for our friends and for this tremendous privilege we have to live and learn and laugh and love and to develop God's grace in our lives.

8

Come Before Winter

If we searched the history of the world for its greatest men, one of those who would stand out most prominently would be Paul, the famous Christian apostle. He was born at Tarsus (see Acts 9:11), educated at the feet of Gamaliel (see Acts 22:3), and after the straightest manner of the Jewish religion, he lived a Pharisee.

As a member of the Sanhedrin, he voted for the persecution of the Christians (see Acts 8:3), and took part in the martyrdom of Stephen (see Acts 7:58). Then one day he started for Damascus to further persecute members of the Church. On the way, the resurrected Jesus appeared to him and completely changed his purpose in being as well as the outcome of his life (see Acts 9:4).

After his baptism by Ananias (see Acts 9:18), Paul retired for a time to Arabia (see Gal. 1:17); and when the time was propitious he began one of the most successful missionary careers of which we have record. He had a long and successful background as a scholar, and he was not a stranger to power; but now these were all subordinated to a career of far greater importance.

In the midst of his heavenly vision, as he stood there trembling and astonished, he said, "Lord, what wilt thou have me to do?" The Lord already had a lot of work marked out for Paul. He said to Ananias,

> He is a chosen vessel unto me . . .
>
> For I will shew him how great things he must suffer for my name's sake. (Acts 9:15-16)

From that day, Paul ceased not to carry forward with the utmost vigor his assigned task. Then, after some thirty years of ministry, he described his manner of life thus:

> In labours more abundant, in stripes above measure, in prisons more frequent, in deaths oft.
>
> Of the Jews five times received I forty stripes save one.

Thrice was I beaten with rods, once was I stoned, thrice I suffered shipwreck, a night and a day I have been in the deep;

In journeyings often, in perils of waters, in perils of robbers, in perils of mine own countrymen, in perils by the heathen, in perils in the city, in perils in the wilderness, in perils in the sea, in perils among false brethren;

In weariness and painfulness, in watchings often, in hunger and thirst, in fastings often, in cold and nakedness.

Beside those things that are without, that which cometh upon me daily, the care of all the churches. (2 Cor. 11:23-28)

Of all of his troubles, this last must have been the most wearisome for Paul—the care that comes from within the Church. It is easy to put up with problems that are on the outside; the real heartbreak comes when the difficulty is from within.

Paul was finally imprisoned in Rome. There he suffered martyrdom when he was beheaded about A.D. 67. The last words Paul ever wrote, so far as we are aware, included his second letter to Timothy written shortly before his death. Timothy was much younger than Paul. His genuine devotion had made him one of Paul's dearest friends.

Paul had not only known Timothy from childhood, but he also knew his grandmother, Lois, and his mother, Eunice, who, like Timothy, were also characterized by their strong faith. Paul refers to Timothy as his "son in the gospel." Timothy was ordained to the ministry under the hands of Paul. Legend also has it that Timothy was the first Bishop of Ephesus.

Paul's last letter was filled with reminders to Timothy to be true and faithful. It also urged Timothy to visit him in his prison in Rome. Paul directed Timothy to stop on the way at the home of Carpus in Troas to pick up the books and parchment Paul had left there. (This request indicates that Paul was a scholar to the very end.)

Paul also asked Timothy to bring the cloak he had left in Troas. It has been said that this cloak had been wet with the brine of the Mediterranean, made white with the snows of Galatia, yellow with the dust of the Egnation Way, and crimson with the blood of Paul's own wounds received in the cause of Christ.

When Paul left his cloak in Troas, he had not expected to spend a dreary winter in the chilly dungeon of a Roman prison. And, inasmuch as the summer was now already waning, Paul needed this extra clothing to keep him warm. Most of all, Paul was hungry for friendship and sympathy. Before he died he wanted to see his son, Timothy, again, to enjoy the warm fellowship of his faithful friend. (To know that you are about to die must be a challenging experience, especially when you have to face it alone.)

In his confinement, Paul had not only been lonely but disappointed as well. Listen to the spirit of discouragement breathed out of his last letter. It says,

All they which are in Asia be turned away from me. (2 Tim. 1:15)

Demas hath forsaken me, having loved this present world, and is departed unto Thessalonica; Crescens to Galatia, Titus unto Dalmatia. (2 Tim. 4:10)

He said,

Alexander the coppersmith did me much evil: the Lord reward him according to his works:

. . . for he hath greatly withstood our words.

At my first answer no man stood with me, but all men forsook me. (2 Tim. 4:14-16)

Paul said, "[I] greatly [desire] to see thee . . . that I may be filled with joy" (2 Tim. 1:4); then he added, "Do thy diligence to come before winter" (2 Tim. 4:21).

There may have been a number of reasons why Paul wanted Timothy to come before winter. First, Paul was now an old man; he needed the support and cheer that Timothy could give him. Besides, he didn't expect that he would be permitted to live much longer as he had written, "For I am now ready to be offered, and the time of my departure is at hand" (2 Tim. 4:6).

In addition, when winter set in, all navigation closed in the Mediterranean. The danger of a ship then venturing out to sea was indicated by the fact that Paul, himself, had been shipwrecked three times and had barely escaped with his life. Naturally, he didn't want Timothy exposed to such a risk in winter time. Therefore, if Timothy didn't come before winter, he couldn't come until spring. Paul also wanted his cloak to keep him warm and his books to keep him company during the long, cold, lonesome winter days and nights that he would be required to spend in prison.

We do not know whether Timothy arrived in time. We would like to think that he did. We would like to think that he started on his way the very day Paul's letter reached him in far away Ephesus. He would have journeyed first to Troas to pick up the books and the cloak. It has been thought that he would probably have sailed past Samothracia to Neapolis and hence by the Egnation Way across the plains of Philippi and on through Macedonia to the Adriatic where he would have taken ship to Brundasium, and then up the Appian Way to Rome and the prison, and Paul.

We might imagine what would have taken place, providing Timothy made it in time. Probably no one could have soothed Paul's troubled spirit as effectively as the disciple whom he so truly loved.

And what a wonderful privilege it would have been for Timothy, himself, to have been with the great Apostle during his last hours of life. What wonderful times they would have had together. Undoubtedly Timothy would have read to Paul from the prized books and parchments that were so important to him, and what joy it would have been for him, in turn, to listen to the wise commentary of Paul.

Certainly Timothy would have helped Paul write his last letters. He would have reassured him in his faith during these hours, may even have walked with him to the place of execution near the pyramid of Cestius. Such an experience would have given Timothy wonderful memories and motives to last for the balance of his life. For, as Longfellow once wrote:

> Were a star quenched on high,
>   For ages would its light
> Still traveling downward from the sky
>   Shine on our mortal sight.
>
> So when a great man dies
>   For years beyond our ken,
> The light he leaves behind him lies
>   Upon the paths of men.

Of course there is always the unpleasant possibility that Timothy did not arrive in time. There are always so many reasons to procrastinate. There are so many distractions to which we may succumb along the way.

Just suppose Timothy did not make it before the Mediterranean winter closed which would have prevented him from traveling. That would mean Paul endured his cold, dreary, dungeon cell alone, without his cloak and without his beloved books. Then Paul would have walked alone, and unsupported, to his place of execution without his beloved disciple's presence or support.

We can well imagine Paul's disappointment as he waited. When Timothy finally arrived, those connected with the prison might have said to him, "So you are Timothy! You are the one he waited for and talked about. Until the very hour he was beheaded, Paul talked of you and hoped that you would get here in time. Every time the jailer put his key in the door, he thought you had arrived. Paul's last message was for you; he said, 'Give my love to my son, Timothy, when he comes.' "

And how Timothy must have grieved that he had not "come before winter." And it really didn't matter now that he had come because the great Apostle had been beheaded.

Timothy might have felt then like the apostles who were too sleepy to watch with Jesus during His long agony in Gethsemane. When the time had passed, and they had failed, Jesus said, "Sleep on now, and take your rest: behold, the hour is at hand, and the Son of man is betrayed" (Matt. 26:45). Sleep is a partial death; sometimes we just sleep on and on forever.

But besides its human interest, there is a constructive parable for our lives in Paul's letter. In the loneliness of his prison cell, Paul laid bare his soul. He pled with Timothy to come before winter. He said:

> My dearly beloved son: Grace, mercy, and peace, from God the Father and Christ Jesus our Lord.
>
> I thank God, whom I serve . . . with pure conscience, that without ceasing I have remembrance of thee in my prayers night and day.
>
> Greatly desiring to see thee, being mindful of thy tears, that I may be filled with joy. (2 Tim. 1:2-4)

Paul knew that his own battle was over. His concern was now for Timothy and the other followers of the Christ who had appeared to him many years before on the Damascus road. Paul said:

> I have fought a good fight, I have finished my course, I have kept the faith:
>
> Henceforth there is laid up for me a crown of righteousness, which the Lord, the righteous judge, shall give me at that day: and not to me only, but unto all them also that love his appearing. (2 Tim. 4:7-8)

We also have certain things that should be done that will not wait—things that will never be done unless they are done "before winter." There are words of love and appreciation that must be spoken before the winter of life sets in. There is character that must be improved and faith that must be vitalized. There are certain duties that cannot be performed just anytime; they must be done during their favorable seasons.

Our lives are rather like hot metal resting in particular molds. If the iron is permitted to cool, it thereafter refuses all other shapes. There are times when life's metal is, as it were, molten and can be worked into any design that is desired. But, if it is permitted to wait out the winter, it cools and tends toward a state of fixation in which it is impossible to do or plan any good works. This hour is the hour of our opportunity; now the chains of our evil habits can be broken. If they are not broken now, they may bind us forever.

There are no instructions in the Bible that say, "Believe in Christ tomorrow," or "Repent and be saved tomorrow." The spirit always says—TODAY! Today is the day of salvation, never tomorrow. This is your hour. Now is the accepted time. If you hear the voice say "Come before winter," do not delay. Harden not your heart. The shortness of your life brings a great urgency upon you. God, Himself, seems to be in a big hurry about some things.

In his last interview with Jonathan, David said, "As thy soul liveth, there is but a step between me and death" (1 Sam. 20:3). This is the story of every man.

There is no moment like the present. If we do not execute our resolution when it is fresh, we may have little hope to do so afterwards; for tomorrow, many hopes will be dissipated, values will be lost, and many good impulses will perish. As James Russell Lowell writes:

> Life is a leaf of paper white
>> Whereon each one of us may write
> His word or two, and then comes night.
>> Greatly begin! though thou have time
> But for a line, be that sublime,—
>> Not failure, but low aim, is crime.

A high aim and a sense of urgency may prevent tardiness and sloth from robbing us of our blessings.

9

The Ransom

There is a legend to the effect that, during the early conquests of Julius Caesar, he was once captured and held for ransom by pirates. During his forty-day confinement, he won their admiration by his coolness, friendliness, and wit. However, when he learned that they had set his ransom at $55,000, he laughed at them. He felt that they did not understand the value of their prisoner.

Caesar suggested to the pirates that they raise their sights. Consequently, the ransom figure was reset at $550,000. He also laughingly promised to crucify each of them as soon as the ransom was paid. This promise he faithfully carried out immediately after his release.

But even $550,000 is a small amount to pay for a Caesar. He put together the mightiest empire ever known in the world up to that time. He developed Rome's military power, improved her government, upgraded her education, and filled her coffers with wealth.

It is interesting to note, however, that these barbarians are not the only ones who have been bad judges of human values. Joseph was sold into Egypt for twenty pieces of silver which was equivalent to eleven American dollars. Then Joseph built granaries and stored up enough corn in the years of plenty to avert the long, hard famine that followed. And thus, for eleven dollars, two nations were saved from starvation.

But Judas Iscariot probably made the biggest miscalculation in human values when he sold Jesus to the Jews for thirty pieces of silver. Jesus became the Savior of the world and the Redeemer of men.

In the Council of Heaven, the Lord was speaking of all people who would live on the earth when He said, "I will ransom them from the power of the grave" (Hosea 13:14). His was the only life with sufficient value to break the bonds of death. He did that which we could not do for ourselves, "For as in Adam all die, even so in Christ shall all be made alive" (1 Cor. 15:22).

But this is not all there is to salvation. The degree of our eternal exaltation depends upon our willingness to repent of our sins and upon our obedience to God's laws. The Lord has said, "For behold, my blood shall not cleanse them if they hear me not" (D&C 29:17).

Our responsibility is indicated in a great revelation which says,

> For behold, I, God, have suffered these things for all, that they might not suffer if they would repent;
> But if they would not repent they must suffer even as I;
> Which suffering caused myself, even God, the greatest of all, to tremble because of pain, and to bleed at every pore, and to suffer both body and spirit—and would that I might not drink the bitter cup, and shrink. (D&C 19:16-18)

The fall of man made us all subject to eternal death; only by shedding the blood of the Son of God could we be redeemed. The price He paid should help us appreciate the fact that our ransom is the most important event that has ever taken place upon this earth. Therefore, in appreciation and gratitude, we join with Charles H. Gabriel in singing his hymn of worship.

> I stand all amazed at the love Jesus offers me,
> Confused at the grace that so fully he proffers me;
> I tremble to know that for me he was crucified,
> That for me, a sinner, he suffered, he bled and died.
> Oh, it is wonderful that he should care for me
>   Enough to die for me!
> Oh, it is wonderful, wonderful to me.
>
> I marvel that he would descend from his throne divine
> To rescue a soul so rebellious and proud as mine;
> That he should extend his great love unto such as I,
> Sufficient to own, to redeem, and to justify.
> Oh, it is wonderful that he should care for me
>   Enough to die for me!
> Oh, it is wonderful, wonderful to me!
>
> I think of his hands pierced and bleeding to pay the debt.
> Such mercy, such love, and devotion can I forget?
> No, no, I will praise and adore at the mercy seat,
> Until at the glorified throne I kneel at his feet.

Oh, it is wonderful that he should care for me
    Enough to die for me!
Oh, it is wonderful, wonderful to me!

This practice of paying ransoms is still big business. Not long ago evil people kidnapped little Bobby Greenlease of Kansas City, Missouri. The kidnappers wrote his parents a letter which said, "We will let you have him back for $600,000." The money was furnished. I am sure that, if they could, the parents would have been willing to pay $600 million or $600 billion dollars to get their son back.

But Jesus placed the value of human life at a much higher price. He compared the worth of one human soul to the wealth of the entire world, which is trillions of dollars.

This word "ransom" has several different meanings. The dictionary says that to ransom is to redeem. It may be the act of releasing a captive by the payment of a consideration. Usually when we owe someone a large debt, we give them a mortgage on our securities. Then, before we can get back a clear title to our property, we must pay any balance outstanding against it. We redeem our lives in about the same way.

The first mortgage is held by our Creator. Paul says, "Ye are not your own . . . ye are bought with a price" (1 Cor. 6:19-20). Under the arrangement made in the Council of Heaven, if we are obedient to God's laws, this mortgage will be paid by the atonement of the great Redeemer. But, for various reasons, most of us pile up other liens against our lives. This must also be paid.

One who commits a crime against the state and doesn't want to be confined in jail is sometimes given the privilege of ransoming himself by paying an equivalent fine in cash. But, one way or another, every law carries a penalty for its violation.

A group of the ancients had an interesting way of punishing crime. If one became a murderer, his punishment was to be chained to the corpse of his victim so that there was no way he could disentangle himself from the result of his evil deed. Wherever he went forevermore he must drag the dead body of his victim with him. If later he should decide to kill again, another corpse would be added to his oppressive burden.

Such a punishment seems severe, yet life has a program of retribution that is closely akin to it. Everyone is chained to his sin. When one violates the law of temperance, a ruinous, driving thirst attaches itself to push him further and further down the road to despair.

The sentence of one who tells lies is that he eventually becomes a liar. If one neglects the laws of learning, a sentence is imposed that he is forever chained to his ignorance. And who can imagine a more dreadful bondage than to be compelled to drag a foul load of sin until the payment is made.

The Apostle Paul probably had this ancient custom in mind when he cried out, "O wretched man that I am! who shall deliver me from the body of this death?" (Rom. 7:24). We might echo, "Who indeed?" Our most serious problem is how we are going to be redeemed from the dreadful bondage of such things as atheism, immorality, dishonesty, and disobedience to God.

The price of redemption from any sin is always terribly high. Think of fortunes that have been lost, the sufferings that have been endured while dragging the oppressive burdens of alcoholism, dishonesty, and drug addiction. It has been said that the best way to break a bad habit is to drop it. But how can we drop nicotine, or indifference, or sin after we have their chains tightly wrapped around us?

A wealthy man would pay a large sum of money to be excused from serving a twenty-year jail sentence under the miserable conditions in any penitentiary. But how much more would it be worth to be bailed out of an eternal sentence in hell? To be ransomed from hell is not only to be relieved of suffering but also to be freed from the depressing company of a miserable group of sinners.

If we actually spent a few months in hell getting a taste of its torments and suffering, the thought of being ransomed, redeemed, and sanctified might have a much greater appeal than at present. If it was worth $550,000 for Caesar to get away from the pirates and live those extra few years in Rome, what would it be worth to us if we could cast off our sins and fully enjoy the comfort, peace of mind, beauty, and happiness of our heavenly home forever?

We ought to get clearly in mind tangible thoughts about how much our own soul is worth. The soul is described in the scriptures as spirit and body when they become inseparably connected. The body is the lesser part of this combination, but even it has tremendous value.

Satan and his followers have been forever denied the privilege of having bodies as a part of the punishment for their ante-mortal rebellion against right. Yet every spirit child of God hungers for a body.

We remember the evil spirits who appeared to Jesus in His day who preferred the bodies of swine to no bodies at all. Worse, Satan and his followers can never hope for redemption. They will be forever denied the exaltation of having a body of flesh and bones.

If such a body were not necessary, it never would have been created. If it were not necessary for eternity, the resurrection would never have been instituted. If a body of flesh and bones were not necessary for God, the Father, then why was God, the Son, resurrected? We would not like to lose a leg or an eye or a brain here; certainly it would be far more terrible to lose them hereafter.

A utility linesman was paralyzed when he came in contact with a live wire. In the lawsuit that followed, he was asked to smile before the jury. Because he could only smile on one side of his face, the jury awarded him $100,000 in damages. If half a smile is worth $100,000, what would a whole smile be worth? But if we are not redeemed, what will there be to smile about?

Suppose we were to get a total value for ourselves by adding up our half-billion-dollar stomach, our three-billion-dollar brain, our two-hundred-thousand-dollar smile; then add an appropriate amount for a couple of billion-dollar-eyes, two willing hands, and a miraculous voice.

To this subtotal, we might credit a few hundred billion dollars for an immortal spirit that will be inseparably joined with a glorified body so that we might have eternal joy. Then suppose this miraculous creation, formed in God's image, is in hock to sin—mortgaged to the hilt in an amount we are completely unable to pay?

Then suppose we were told about this magnificent atonement made by the Son of God, told that the price had already been paid so that our lives could be ransomed, redeemed, glorified, celestialized, and eternalized, and in every way fully qualified to live forever with God in eternal glory. Who can even comprehend the value of the peace, happiness, and joy of this situation?

Then suppose we ask ourselves what we would be willing to do to bring this about. One of the best facts of life is that we may have every blessing we are willing to live for. Even now Satan may be laughing at us because we don't know our own value as the children and heirs of the eternal God.

But some of us still go blindly on our way, plastering one mortgage on top of another until we are so deep in bondage that His blood will not cleanse us. Caesar crucified his captives, but Satan has a far worse fate in store for his captives. And all who remain forever unredeemed may fall into his hands. Even the fires of hell may not be able to burn out the dross.

We don't need to wait until eternity to get started on this most important project of redemption. We operate now under a kind of lend-lease arrangement; only after this life is finished will we be turned over to ourselves and have eternal glory added upon our heads forever and ever.

Meantime, we can redeem ourselves from ignorance through study. We can redeem ourselves from sloth through self-motivation. We can redeem ourselves from sin by repentance and self-mastery, and the great Redeemer will pay the ransom for our souls, if we are obedient to Him.

A significant idea of our world is that through the great literature, including the inspirational scriptures, and through our own thoughtfulness, we may learn of our own values and what we can do to ransom ourselves from death and inherit all of the benefits made available to us.

10

Meditations of Marcus Aurelius

Marcus Aurelius, born in Rome A.D. 121, was one of the greatest of the Roman emperors. He was given the name of Marcus Annius Verus; but later, in the year A.D. 138, when he was seventeen, he was adopted by the Roman Emperor, Titus Aurelius Antonious.

Marcus Aurelius was educated by the orator Fronto, but later he turned aside from rhetoric to the study of stoic philosophy, of which he was the last distinguished representative. His meditations, which he wrote in Greek, are among the most noteworthy expressions of this system of philosophy.

The precepts of his meditations were recorded in his writings and carried out by him in his own life with singular consistency. In his public and his private life, he was conscientious to the highest degree.

Marcus became Emperor in the year A.D. 161, when he was forty years old. Marcus Aurelius, and his predecessor emperor, are noted as the only Roman emperors who ruled with an eye single to the welfare of their subjects. His reign, though marked by justice and moderation at home, was troubled by constant warfare on the frontiers of the empire. He spent much of his later years in the uncongenial task of commanding armies that no longer proved invincible against the barbaric hoards.

During those fatiguing campaigns, Marcus endured all the hardships incident to a rigorous climate and a military life with the patience and serenity which did the highest honor to his philosophy. That is, Marcus Aurelius practiced in his life those things he meditated upon and preached about to others. His reign as emperor lasted for nineteen years, and he died in the year A.D. 180 at age fifty-nine from a pestilential disease which prevailed in the army.

Even though he gained acclaim for the way he conducted his military life, he is probably remembered more now for his meditations. Twelve volumes contain ideas jotted down by him from time to time in leisure moments, and while he was in camp along the Danube during his campaign against barbaric hoards.

The dictionary says that a meditation is a process of "thinking to a purpose." The word meditation is related to other great words such as "thinking," "study," and "pondering."

These twelve volumes of meditations are made up of scholarly collections of maxims and thoughts in the spirit of stoic philosophy, which, without much connection of skill in composition, leave the pure sentiments of piety and benevolence. They picture, with faithfulness, the mind and character of this noblest of Roman emperors. Simple in style and sincere in tone, they record for all time the height reached by pagan aspiration in its effort to solve the problems of human behavior and conduct; and the essential agreement between his practice with his teaching proved that "even in a palace, life may be well lived."

Since the death of Marcus Aurelius, several translations and abbreviations of his works have been made from the original Greek language in which they were first written. Through the centuries, one of the world's most famous and inspirational books has remained with various translations usually condensed into one volume. We know these writings now as *The Meditations of Marcus Aurelius.*

No one seems certain whether these thoughts were intended by Marcus for eyes other than his own. They are fragmentary notes of his reflections in battle, his meditations on personal improvement of life as well as the government of the vast Roman Empire of which he was the head.

By his writings, and the thinking he did in connection therewith, he kept alive in himself the truths learned from historic teachers who taught him in his youth as well as others from whom he learned throughout his life. Certainly his writings helped him to nerve himself for the enormous tasks he was called upon to perform as head of this great empire as well as fashioning him to be one of the outstanding men of his era.

He was a great student of biography and human personality. In his writings, he often made scholarly lists of virtues, procedures, and success ideas learned from other people. He also wrote down his own ambitions and the pros and cons of his own reasoning powers on the questions with which his life was confronted.

The uplifting effect his life and philosophies had on his subjects and friends might be judged by the fact that his death occasioned universal mourning. Without waiting for the usual decree on the occasion, the Roman Senate and the Roman people voted him a god by acclamation. His image was, long afterward, regarded with peculiar veneration.

We might learn much from this man who has been thought by many to be the greatest emperor the Roman Empire ever had.

Following are a few quotations by which Marcus Aurelius advanced to a position of excellence that caused his subjects to feel that he was ready for godhood.

1. From my grandfather, Verus, I learned good morals and the government of my temper.

2. From the reputation and remembrance of my father, I learned modesty and a manly character.

3. From my mother, piety, beneficence, and abstinence, not only from evil deeds, but even from evil thoughts; and further simplicity in my way of living, far removed from the habits of the rich.

4. From my governor, to be neither of the green nor of the blue party at the game in the Circus, nor a partisan either of the Parmularius or the Scutarius at the gladiator's fights; from him, too, I learned endurance of labor, and to want little, and to work with my own hands, and not to meddle with other people's affairs, and not to be ready to listen to slander.

5. From Diognetus, not to busy myself about trifling things, nor to give myself up passionately to such things; and to endure freedom of speech; and to have become intimate with philosophy; and to have written dialogues in my youth.

6. From Rusticus, I received the impression that my character required improvement and discipline; and from him I learned not to be led astray to sophistic emulation, for to showing myself off as a man who practices much discipline, or does benevolent acts in order to make a display; to read carefully, and not to be satisfied with a superficial understanding of a book; and I am indebted to him for being acquainted with the discourses of Epictetus, which he communicated to me out of his own collection.

7. From Apollonius, I learned freedom of will and undeviating steadiness of purpose; and to look to nothing else, not even

for a moment, except to reason; and to be always the same, in sharp pains, on the occasion of the loss of a child, and in long illness; and to see clearly in a living example that the same man can be both most resolute and yielding, and not peevish in giving his instruction; and to have had before my eyes a man who clearly considered his experience and his skill in expounding philosophical principles as the smallest of his merits; and from him I learned how to receive from friends what are esteemed favours, without being either humbled by them or letting them pass unnoticed.

8. From Sextus, a benevolent disposition, and the example of a family governed in a fatherly manner, and the idea of living conformable to nature and gravity without affection, and to look carefully after the interests of friends, and to tolerate ignorant persons, and those who form opinions without consideration: he had the power of readily accommodating himself to all, so that intercourse with him was more agreeable than any flattery; and at the same time he was most highly venerated by those who associated with him; and he had the faculty both of discovering and ordering in an intelligent and methodical way, the principles necessary for life; and he could express approbation without noisy display, and he possessed much knowledge without ostentation.

9. From Alexander, the grammarian, to refrain from faultfinding, and not in a reproachful way to chide those who uttered any barbarous or solecistic or strange-sounding expression; but dexterously to introduce the very expression which ought to have been used, and in the way of answer or giving confirmation, or joining in an inquiry about the thing itself, not about the work, or by some other fit suggestion.

10. From Fronto, I learned to observe that envy and duplicity and hypocrisy are in a tyrant.

11. To the gods I am indebted for having good grandfathers, good parents, a good sister, good teachers, good associates, good kinsmen and friends, nearly everything good. I thank the gods for giving me such a brother who was able by his moral character to rouse me to vigilance over myself and who, at the same time, pleased me by his respect and affection.

Other meditations recorded by Marcus Aurelius:

1. We are made for cooperation, like feet, like hands, like eyelids, like the rows of the upper and lower teeth.

2. Thou art an old man, no longer let yourself be a slave, no longer let yourself be pulled by the strings like a puppet, no longer be either dissatisfied with thy present lot.

3. Those who do not observe the movements of their own minds must, of necessity, be unhappy.

It would be wise for us to give consideration to the recorded wisdom of Marcus Aurelius.

The Lord recommends meditation, pondering, and thoughtfulness throughout the holy scriptures. The brain has some of the same characteristics as muscle: it is strengthened by the right exercise. Poetry comes out of the meditations of the poet. Philosophy results from meditations of the lover of wisdom. Science is formed in the mind of the inventor.

In fact, all down through the ages, we have had counsel of the great God of creation on the advisability for meditation. At Hiram, Ohio, on February 16, 1832, the Prophet Joseph Smith and Sidney Rigdon received what the Apostle Melvin J. Ballard referred to as the greatest revelation ever given to any people in any age. The Prophet told how this revelation came about. He said:

And while we meditated upon these things, the Lord touched the eyes of our understandings and they were opened, and the glory of the Lord shone round about (D&C 76:19).

It is likely that before God can effectively touch the eyes of our understanding, we ourselves need to do a little meditation to prepare for revelations that come from Him.

On many occasions, He said such things as, "Think on these things," or "Ponder on these things." An old proverb says, "God helps those who help themselves." If we want to get God completely on our side, we'd better start on a good program of meditating, thinking, and pondering on those philosophies of life He has approved by which He can most effectively bless our lives.

Following are quotations on meditation taken from the scriptures. The Lord said to Joshua:

This book of the law shall not depart out of thy mouth; but thou shalt meditate therein day and night, that thou mayest observe to do according to all that is written therein: for then thou shalt . . . have good success. (Joshua 1:8)

King David said to the Lord, "Give ear to my words, O Lord, consider my meditation" (Psalm 5:1).

Meditation may actually have more significance in our lives than do our prayers. David combined his prayers and meditation together as he said, "Let the words of my mouth, and the meditation of my heart, be acceptable in thy sight, O Lord, my strength, and my redeemer" (Psalm 19:14).

David also combined his meditations with gratitude and several other things when he said,

> Thus will I bless thee while I live: I will lift up my hands in thy name.
>
> My soul shall be satisfied as with marrow and fatness; and my mouth shall priase thee with joyful lips:
>
> When I remember thee upon my bed, and meditate on thee in my night watches. (Psalm 63:4-6)

Again David said,

> I will meditate also of all thy work, and talk of thy doings. (Psalm 77:12)
>
> My meditation of him shall be sweet: I will be glad in the Lord. (Psalm 104:34)
>
> I have more understanding than all my teachers: for thy testimonies are my meditation. (Psalm 119:99)
>
> I remember the days of old; I meditate on all thy works; I muse on the work of thy hands. (Psalm 143:5)

In his letter to Timothy, Paul said, "Meditate upon these things: give thyself wholly to them; that thy profiting may appear to all" (1 Tim. 4:15).

The Lord has said that man is that he might have joy. This is not brought about by meditations of sin and depression nor of feeling the miseries of the damned; rather we ought to meditate with David when he said, "This is the day which the Lord hath made; we will rejoice and be glad in it" (Psalm 118:24). Before we are able to *be* happy, we must *feel* happy.

11

Come Thou . . . into the Ark

Just before the crucifixion, Jesus was telling His disciples about signs that would immediately precede His glorious second coming to judge the world. Among other interesting things He said:

> As the days of Noe [Noah] were, so shall also the coming of the Son of man be.
>
> For as in the days that were before the flood they were eating and drinking, marrying and giving in marriage, until the day that Noe [Noah] entered into the ark,
>
> And knew not until the flood came, and took them all away; so shall also the coming of the Son of man be. (Matt. 24:37-39)

Inasmuch as we are one of those principals involved in this comparison, it might be well to reread, occasionally, the account of the days of Noah and the flood, to try to get the feeling and the picture of what it was like to have been an actual participant in such an event. If we could catch the spirit of what happened in Noah's day, we could better prepare ourselves for what is ahead of us.

Apparently Noah's day was quite a day. The Bible says there were many mighty men, and men of great renown living on the earth in those days. Like our own day, these important people were busy with the accomplishments and pleasures of their time. But, like us, they had also turned their attention away from God. Their slogan was, "Let us eat, drink, and be merry for tomorrow we die."

William James reminds us that "only that which holds our attention determines our action." In Noah's time, the people's attention was centered on the wrong things. As in the world of our own day, wickedness was the basic problem. The Lord was so grieved about this that He finally said, "I will destroy man whom I have created" (Moses 8:26). It is supposed He felt that everybody's interest would be best served by making a new start.

Of all the people on the earth at that time, only Noah seemed to find favor with the Lord. He was sent by Him to warn the others to turn from their unrighteousness. For one hundred and twenty years Noah tried to get these people to change their ways, to believe in God. But he was not successful.

Finally their time ran out. Then God said to Noah, "The end of all flesh is come before me, for the earth is filled with violence, and behold I will destroy all flesh from off the earth" (Moses 8:30).

Then God commanded Noah to build an ark in which he and his family might be saved. God gave detailed instructions as to the ark's size, exactly how it should be built, and what should be taken inside. So Noah went to work building a great ship even though he had no water to float it on.

People thought it was ridiculous for Noah to build his ship on dry ground. It would have been a lot easier for them to have believed in a flood during the rainy season. Noah's ark was built for a flood no one believed in. This must have provided an interesting and humorous topic of conversation. No doubt many curious folks made excursions out to Noah's house to see the great ship that had no water to sail on.

But finally the ark was finished and stocked with food. The animals were taken aboard. Everything was in readiness for the great event which the prophet had foretold. The cup of iniquity of the people was nearly full; a world-wide cataclysm was trembling on the brink of its fulfillment even though as yet it had not even begun to sprinkle.

The people carried on their business as usual during that period of calm that always precedes a storm.

This period was comparable to our own day. Our world is again balancing on the brink of another catastrophe of even greater proportions because of our evil. We should know how much the Lord dislikes sin. Of our own day the Lord has said:

> For the hour is nigh and the day soon at hand when the earth is ripe; and all the proud and they that do wickedly shall be as stubble; and I will burn them up, saith the Lord of Hosts, that wickedness shall not be upon the earth. (D&C 29:9)

We are aware that at any moment our present peaceful calm may give way to the awful calamity of fire and destruction that may be unloosed upon us. In our day, as well as in Noah's, the people have been warned. But it was easy for the antediluvians to be unconcerned as long as the sun was shining just as it is so easy for us to shrug our shoulders and say, "I do not believe."

When the ark was ready, and the fateful hour had struck, the Lord said to Noah, "Come, thou and all thy house into the ark." When Noah and his family were inside, the record says, "And the Lord shut him in" (Gen. 7:16). When the door had been fastened, and everything was in readiness, it began to sprinkle. Probably just a few drops at first, because no one was even slightly concerned. It had sprinkled before. Undoubtedly they joked about Noah's warning prophecy and their own need for moisture, but everyone felt sure there would not be enough rain to do any damage. But soon the rain began in earnest. It kept getting worse with no sign of any letup.

We might try to imagine the look on the faces of the people when they began to realize that this was no ordinary rain. We have been told that the clouds thickened, the heavens grew darker, the water poured down in torrents. Creeks and rivers were soon overflowing their banks. People started looking for the safety of higher ground. They weren't joking now about Noah or the moisture. They knew that things were rapidly getting out of hand.

Then the storm struck with all its fury. It must have seemed that the elements had gone wild. The Bible says, "[That] same day were all the fountains of the great deep broken up, and the windows of heaven were opened" (Gen. 7:11). Terror and confusion reigned.

People who had derided the old preacher were now desperately trying to save their lives. Some undoubtedly reached the top of the hills. But the storm was sweeping the highest ground. Lightnings flashed, the thunders reverberated through the dreadful gloom. Winds wailed and moaned an accompaniment to the agonies of a dying world. Hills, mountains, the earth itself trembled. Rocks and buildings crashed in convulsions as civilizations' doom was being sealed by the bursting heavens.

If Noah had been around now to talk to them about repenting, the people might have been more willing to give him a few minutes of their time. But it was too late for repentance. Noah was in the ark: they were on the outside.

Sinful inhabitants of the earth, white with horror, were now making hasty preparations to die. With what awful terror must they have heard the screams, the calls, the prayers of helpless neighbors and friends. Already dead bodies of men and beasts were floating everywhere. Waters kept rising until no place of safety could be found. Finally the tops of the highest mountains were reached. Scripture says:

And the waters prevailed exceedingly upon the earth; and all the high hills, that were under the whole heaven, were covered.

Fifteen cubits upward did the waters prevail; and the mountains were covered.

And all flesh died that moved upon the earth, both of fowl, and of cattle, and of beast . . . and every man. (Gen. 7:19-21)

What a fearful thing when man brings such dreadful destruction upon himself by his own thoughtlessness and disobedience.

Of all of the people upon the earth, only Noah and his family remained alive. The ark had risen with the water and was riding the crest of the flood above the carcasses of a dead world. Noah, the man of faith who had prepared an ark to the saving of his house, was floating safely upon the bosom of the flood.

As the ark had risen, many of Noah's friends undoubtedly would like to have signaled him to bring the ark past their housetop to take them aboard. But after God had shut the door of the ark, it was too late. Noah was locked in. Everyone else was locked out.

But what about us and our day? Jesus indicated that history would repeat itself: that "as the days of Noe [Noah] were, so shall also the coming of the Son of man be" (Matt. 24:37). We have been warned that the earth will be cleansed by fire. According to the scripture, the catastrophe reserved for our day may make Noah's flood seem like a summer picnic.

Suppose that Noah had provided his children with a good college education and a life annuity but failed to prepare them to enter the ark. What a pitiful sight it would have been to see Noah sailing away in the ark, leaving his children behind. Shem, Ham, and Japheth got into the ark because their parents took them in. Other children did not make it because their parents' interests were elsewhere.

A lady and her three children once boarded a ship bound for Australia. The ship was sunk. The mother sent a two-word telegram to her husband: "Saved alone."

It is a tragedy in any age for parents to be saved by themselves. An ancient American prophet said, "As I partook of the fruit . . . I began to be desirous that my family should partake of it also" (1 Nephi 8:12).

Some of our strongest desires are for our family's welfare; while we are anxious to start our children out in life with a financial nest egg, we would also do well to keep an eye open to getting them into the ark of their eternal salvation. God said to Noah, "Come thou and all thy house into the ark" (Gen. 7:1).

We might think of the ark as a type of the saving powers of Christ: it is a type of His church. There is only one place in the world today where we and our children can be safe: that is in the fold of Christ, living in obedience to His commandments. Righteousness is the only condition that can ride out the waves of death and hell.

Once Noah and his family were in the ark, they were safe. No flood could swallow them then. Speaking of the place of our own present safety, the Savior has told us, "I am the door." Then He added, "No man cometh unto the Father, but by me" (John 14:6).

He gave us one of the signs of His glorious second coming, and the end of the world as we know it, when He said that His "gospel of the kingdom shall be preached in all the world for a witness unto all nations; and then shall the end come" (Matt. 24:14). That warning cry is going forth. Men and women are asked to believe and obey the saving principles of the gospel.

What a great privilege that we may accept God's invitation to come into the ark, that through our obedience we and our families may find safety when pending troubles break over the world.

12

Some Cords That Bind Us Together

In 1851, Herman Melville wrote a whaling story entitled, *Moby Dick*. In his book, Mr. Melville pictures the lives of whale hunters as they hunted and killed whales. Because whale hunters are human beings, it is interesting to read about the way they lived, about what they thought and did.

A whale hunt was a mutual undertaking which usually lasted about three years. At the end of the journey, profits from the hunt were distributed among the participants according to a formula previously agreed on.

The whaling ship in Mr. Melville's story was the *Pequod*, with Captain Ahab in command. The captain was a very unusual person. On one voyage he lost one of his legs in a fight with a great white whale named "Moby Dick." He dedicated his life thereafter to finding and destroying this mammoth creature that roamed the world's oceans. In their final encounter, Captain Ahab lost his life to Moby Dick.

Even a land-lover may gain interesting and profitable experiences from reading Mr. Melville's book. In this vicarious experience, we have the adventure without the risk. We may profit from the experiences of many people without the loss of time and treasure which they suffered. We might also get some good from the interesting philosophies Mr. Melville builds around his characters since they amplify many common interests of our own lives.

In their experiences we may also see exposed our own complexes and human weaknesses as well as the foolish sins to which our own flesh is heir. On the other hand, we may recognize some of our own potential strengths and abilities.

To hunt a whale is a big undertaking. The whale is the largest creature on this earth. Because it is dangerous to challenge a whale, a whale hunter had better have aboard an ample supply of courage and real skill.

When a whale is killed, it is floated alongside the whaling vessel and stripped of its blubber, which is the outside layer, serving the whale both as a skin and an overcoat. The blubber is said to resemble fine-grained beef, except that it is much tougher. It may vary from eight to fifteen inches in thickness, and it contains the valuable oils for which the whale is sought.

After the whale's body is securely fastened to the whaling boat, blubber is stripped off by a hazardous process. One of the two men who performs this operation is called the stripper. He is armed with a cutting spade and stands on the whale itself. As most of the whale is submerged in the water, the top of the whale lies a little below the level of the ship's deck so that the workman who stands on the whale's back is exposed to many hazards.

For one thing, the whale is very slippery. If the stripper slips on one side, he may be crushed between the whale and the ship. If he slips on the other side, the large company of vicious sharks that have gathered to get a few free meals at the expense of the dead, helpless whale would make short work of a stripper who loses his footing and falls among them.

To make the work of the whale stripper a little safer, the man standing on the whale's back is given a partner who stands on the ship's deck. The man on the deck is also equipped with a long-handled cutting spade, enabling him to fight off sharks that might come too close to his friend on the whale's back. Another safety factor is provided by connecting the two men together with what is called a "monkey rope," a title probably borrowed from the old organ grinder who went around playing his portable organ. A monkey on the end of a rope had a collection cup to gather money for the organ grinder.

In the process of collecting the blubber, one end of the monkey rope was securely fastened to a broad canvas belt worn by the man on the back of the whale. The other was fastened to a similar belt worn by his partner on the deck of the ship. Then, for better or for worse, these two men were inseparably joined together until their job was done.

If, during this period, the man who worked on the whale's back should slip off and sink to rise no more, the one on the deck had to share his fate. That is, if the one on the deck could not prevent his friend from being lost, then both custom and honor demanded that he also must die. It would be completely dishonorable for him to cut the rope in an attempt to save only himself.

This union could not be dissolved, even with the clause we sometimes insert in our marriage contracts which says, "until death do us part." The unseverable cord was the best idea the whale hunters could devise as a guarantee to the stripper that his partner on the deck would be absolutely faithful. This responsibility would stir up in each one the greatest possible desire to protect his partner.

The man on the whale's back carried a double responsibility: one careless act could destroy him and pull his innocent partner down to equal disaster. Characters in *Moby Dick* had many close calls. Sometimes the rope jerked so hard that only with all their mighty effort were they able to prevent themselves from sliding into the sea. Thus they watched out for each other.

This relationship reminds us of mountain climbers who tie themselves together with a kind of monkey rope so that if one slips, the others have a chance either to prevent his fall or to share his fate. Mountain climbers also tie themselves together as a means of discouraging each other from giving up too easily on the quest and turning back.

As we ponder our own lives, we might think of situations where we have a kind of monkey-rope involvement with others. Whether we are stripping a whale, or living a life, there is an elongated cord that binds each of us to other mortals and immortals. No matter what our circumstances, no one lives unto himself alone; no one dies unto himself alone. There are always those to whom we are inseparably bound.

During the prenatal months of life, every child is joined to the mother by a miraculous umbilical cord. If the mother should make a slip in her high responsibilities to the child she carries by becoming a drug addict or having an abortion, the child will be dragged overboard with her. This cord is severed at birth, yet there are other cords of influence, love, loyalty, need, and service that immediately take its place.

One manifestation of this continued connection is described by Edgar A. Guest as follows:

> A father and his tiny son
> Walked through the streets one stormy day.
> "See, Father," cries the little one,
> "I stepped in your steps all the way."

Ah! random childish hands that deal
Quick thrusts no coat of proof could stay.
It touched him as a point of steel.
"I stepped in your steps all the way."

But those who cast off greed and fear,
Who love and watch, who toil and pray,
How their hearts carol as they hear:
"I stepped in your steps all the way."

Jesus applied the partner relationship by sending His missionaries out two by two: they help prevent each other from falling away or from turning back. God did much the same thing through the marital relationship. He ordained that each man should be bound eternally to a female companion in order to create life, as well as to be responsible for it afterward.

The Lord has said:

For this cause shall a man leave father and mother, and shall cleave to his wife: and they twain shall be one flesh?

. . . What therefore God hath joined together, let not man put asunder. (Matt. 19:5-6)

While they are thus joined together, they may either save the other's life or drag the other down to death.

There is a verse that says:

As the husband is, the wife is.
If thou art mated to a clown
Then the coarseness of his nature
Cannot help but drag thee down.

This cord that binds them together also includes places for the children to be. Thus are sins of the parents visited upon their children. It has been said that the first question God will ask every parent is, "Where are your children?" Just suppose we are not able to give very good answers to that question.

What would God think if the mountain climbers returned home with the rope cut proving that one member had purposely been allowed to fall to his death? Suppose one parent doesn't reach the journey's end. God will probably make a searching inquiry of the parent present regarding the whereabouts of the parent missing.

This is like the responsibility of the ancient Chinese. Tradition had it that when one person saved the life of another, he became forever responsible for the life he had saved. By this monkey-rope idea, teacher and student are tied together. Patient is tied to doctor in that when a doctor makes a bad decision, the patient dies.

John Donne wrote:

> No man is an island, entire of itself, every man is a piece of the continent, a part of the main; [if any part of the continent] be washed away by the sea, [then every man is the loser by just that much.] . . . any man's death diminishes me, because I am involved in mankind.

Members of the family, the community, the country, and the world are all tied together by a long, strong monkey rope. If part of America is destroyed, it is also our funeral, for we are dependent on each other.

Anciently, when a Roman soldier enlisted in the service of Caesar, he made a pledge to hold the life of Caesar dearer than all else. When the emperor's life was threatened, the soldier either had to protect him or fight to the death for him.

Then there is the most important of all ties influencing our success, happiness, and life. There is a great umbilical cord by which we are all connected with God. He has said, "I am the way, the truth, and the life: no man cometh unto the Father, but by me" (John 14:6).

The dictionary says that one meaning attached to the term "umbilical cord" indicates a strong lifeline connecting an astronaut to his vehicle. When he is walking in space outside his vehicle, it supplies him with air and communication. If that cord were cut, the astronaut would be lost in the vast blackness of space.

The dictionary says that a lifeline is a line that can be shot from a vessel in distress at sea by which a strong towline is taken on board another vessel to save the stricken vessel. There is also a lifeline that can be stretched through the surf for bathers to cling to if they need to be rescued. Sometimes a lifeline is also attached to a diver's helmet so that he may be raised or lowered after he is in the water. He may also receive his air supply and communications through this lifeline.

God has thrown us a lifeline; if we keep a strong enough grip on that cord that binds us to Him, we are safe. If we let go, or allow the cord to be cut, we are lost. What a tremendous situation we find ourselves in when God handles the other end of our lifeline! If we slip once in awhile, He will pull us up.

The scriptures tell of a woman whose daughter was possessed of an evil spirit. In agony the mother came to Jesus and said, "Have mercy on me, oh Lord . . . my daughter is grievously vexed with a devil" (Matt. 15:22).

Jesus told the woman that His mission was only to the lost sheep of the house of Israel. But although she was not an Israelite, she would not be put off. She continued to cry, "Have mercy on me." She was suffering for the affliction of her daughter. She did not say to Jesus, "Help my daughter." She said, "Help me." She didn't say, "My daughter is suffering"; she said, "I am suffering."

Then, in granting the blessing she sought, Jesus said to her, "Be it unto thee even as thou wilt" (Matt. 15:28). And her daughter was made whole from that very hour. Jesus didn't say, "Be it unto your daughter as thou wilt," but He said, "Be it unto thee even as thou wilt." The mother's suffering was relieved only when her child had been cured.

Think of the suffering we could lift from others if we cleansed ourselves of evil, for not only God and our parents, but everyone else suffers for our sins.

13

The Last Days of Pompeii

One of the most unusual cities of the world is the ancient city of Pompeii, a Roman city that died during an eruption of Mount Vesuvius on August 24, in the year A.D. 79. Her people were literally buried alive by the rain of pumice and volcanic ash that was spewed over the city by the erupting volcano.

After the forty-eight-hour eruption, Pompeii lay under twenty feet of ashes and lava chunks. Seventeen centuries added another twenty feet of dirt. The volcano had changed the shore line so the city was all but forgotten until the year 1748, when a peasant digging a well over Pompeii made finds which stimulated excavation attempts.

In 1755, Charles III dug into public buildings, and Pompeii sprang to life as the most famous archaeological site in the world for its buried treasures, its historical data, its life-like reality, and an immortal uniqueness unknown to any other city.

In the 19th century, Lord Lytton stimulated general interest by writing his classic, *The Last Days of Pompeii*. He pictured Pompeii in her final hours, before the eruption, as a city for the wealthy people of Rome. Many famous Romans built villas there by the sea in the glamour of Greek elegance.

The people of Pompeii built low, single-family houses of stone, brick, and stucco. They turned blank walls to the streets so that each house looked in on an interior open court called an atrium. This airy atrium was the heart of the Pompeian home, usually guarded by a graceful little statue of the household god. He was saluted with a morning prayer, then an offering was made from the table to encourage him to keep the family healthy, prosperous, and fruitful.

Treasures and jewelry were highly prized and were often taken with their owners to their tombs. Pear trees, cypress, pomegranates, and oleanders grew in profusion in the gardens, and householders planted rose bushes and violets beside their fountains.

A man too poor to afford a large domestic establishment usually hired a painter to portray an imitation garden on the walls of his smaller home. But frescoes of one kind or another were everywhere in Pompeii. Some thirty-five hundred of them can still be seen today. Rich people commissioned artists to paint hundreds of elaborate scenes, many of which are now located in museums of art. More paintings have survived from this ancient city of Pompeii than from all of the rest of the classic world put together.

The main street led to the forum, which was the center of the city's life. Merchants thrived from various trades. Citizens ate and drank well as they reclined on sloping shelves around movable tables. They rose at dawn and went to bed shortly after sunset. About half their days were holidays during which they patronized gladitorial contests or went to the theater or the temple.

Women of Pompeii were very fond of jewelry. They collected rings and brooches, gold bracelets, pins and jeweled buttons. But on that fateful day of August 24, A.D. 79, everything in Pompeii was changed by the four-thousand-foot mountain that stood brooding behind her, preparing to explode. Eruptions were preceded by tremors and muted roarings. Horses and cattle became uneasy, birds fell silent, some flew away.

Just before noon it happened—an ominous shudder shook the ground. Ashes and smoke billowed from the throat of the mountain. Many people ran screaming toward the sea, but most of them stayed. They were buried and preserved in their own homes. The better homes were scarcely injured by the ashes and pumice that preserved them for our day.

At the time Vesuvius blew up, Pliny the Younger was visiting his uncle across the bay in Naples. He recorded the scene in his famous letter to Tacitus. He wrote: "There was a cloud like an umbrella pine which rose to a great height on a sort of trunk and then split off into branches. When night fell, broad sheets of fire and leaping flames blazed at several points."

Few things in our world are more common than the deaths of cities. Almost all of the great civilizations of history have now passed away. Many of them have left no trace of ever having been. The Bible mentions the civilization of Noah's day that was overcome by the flood. But, except for the Bible, nothing is left to tell us about it.

A rainstorm of fire and brimstone wiped out Sodom and Gomorrah. The once mighty nation of Babylon also disappeared from the earth. Nations that have lived and died on our own land have left only crumbling ruins and a few hieroglyphics to tell of their civilization.

But, in the dead city of Pompeii, most of its people were still in their homes as though they were still going on with their work when the volcano erupted. Cook stoves were found with loaves of bread still in the ovens. Half-eaten meals preserved in the ashes were still on the tables.

Last days are always very important. Last days are the key days. Last days judge all of the other days. You could never judge a civilization—or a life—without knowing of its last days. The lives of Judas Iscariot, or Jesus of Nazareth, would lack much of their significance without their last days. Our own last days will also stand out as our most important days. That will be true of the earth itself.

It is interesting that everyone wants to know how things are going to finish. In any of the races of life, the largest congregation always assembles as near as possible to the finish line. In many sporting events, they record the finish on television so that it can be rerun to let everyone know how the contestants finished.

There is an interesting scriptural account of the last days which tells about a man who spent his life accumulating wealth. Finally, when he had no space left to store his goods, he said to himself, "I will pull down my barns, and build greater; and there will I bestow my fruits and my goods. And I will say to my soul, Soul, thou hast much goods laid up for many years; take thine ease, eat, drink and be merry" (Luke 12:18-19).

But God said unto him, "Thou fool, this night thy soul shall be required of thee: then whose shall those things be, which thou hast provided?" (Luke 12:20).

It doesn't matter very much how big our barns are if we are poor toward God when we reach the finish line. No one will ask what kind of starts we made; the only thing most people will be interested in is how we finish. This interest gives an added importance to our last days.

Lord Lytton has aroused our concern over the *Last Days of Pompeii*. But there is every indication that we are now on the threshold of the greatest of all sets of last days as they apply to our own earth.

Our earth is already groaning and trembling with trouble. We are already aware of tremors and muted roarings beneath our feet. All nature is uneasy with its wars, its earthquakes, and its great tribulations. All of the earth's people have a sense of danger, fear, and foreboding. Signs of the times indicate that some shocking devastation is about to take place.

We feel sorry for the people of Pompeii whose remains were preserved by being packed in volcanic ashes for one thousand eight hundred and eighty-eight years; we can imagine how helpful it might have been if they had known in advance about the plans of Mount Vesuvius, with its insides filled with lava and fire, ready to belch out and over them. However, a clear warning did not seem to help the people of Noah's day very much. And only Lot and his family were willing to leave Sodom when the angels told the dwellers therein that everything would be destroyed.

But our most important question is—what about ourselves? Our own last days have not only been foretold, but almost every detail has been written for us to read in advance.

In speaking of our time, Paul said to Timothy:

> This know also, that in the last days perilous times shall come.
> For men shall be lovers of their own selves, covetous, boasters, proud, blasphemers, disobedient to parents, unthankful, unholy,
> Without natural affection, trucebreakers, false accusers, incontinent, fierce, despisers of those that are good,
> Traitors, heady, highminded, lovers of pleasures more than lovers of God;
> Having a form of godliness, but denying the power thereof. (2 Tim. 3:1-5)

Paul says:

> From such turn away. (2 Tim. 3:5)

No wonder, for this in itself ought to be enough to cause an explosion.

Peter also talks about those things that have always triggered explosions when he says:

> Knowing this first, that there shall come in the last days scoffers, walking after their own lusts. (2 Pet. 3:3)

Jesus Himself looked to our day and told of wars and troubles that should immediately precede His second coming to the earth. The last days of the earth, as we have known it, are upon us; they are our most important days.

All the prophets seem to have been given divine knowledge concerning our day. One of the most widely discussed subjects in all of the scriptures is that great event when Christ shall come with His holy angels in flaming fire to cleanse the world of its sin, and to take care of its unfinished business. This is when most of our important events will take place.

At the second coming a main part of the resurrection will take place. Christ will inaugurate His own millennial reign upon the earth. This will be followed by the final judgment and the glorification of the earth. This would not be a very good time to be packed in ashes.

Jacob predicted what would happen to his own posterity in the last days (see Gen. 49:10). The scattered children of Israel will be gathered in the last days. The lost ten tribes will be restored. The gospel of Christ will be preached as a witness unto all nations (see Matt. 24:14). Isaiah seemed almost to have lived in our day.

The Lord even showed to King Nebuchadnezzar what would happen in the last days. Daniel called it "the time of the end," and he predicted our great knowledge explosion. He foresaw the time when all earthly thrones would be cast down and Adam, the ancient of days—or the oldest man—would, under Christ, be the leader of his posterity. (See Dan. 7:9-10.)

The Apostle Peter quoted the words of Joel saying:

> And it shall come to pass in the last days, saith God, I will pour out of my Spirit upon all flesh: and your sons and your daughters shall prophesy, and your young men shall see visions, and your old men shall dream dreams:
>
> And I will shew wonders in heaven above, and signs in the earth beneath; blood, and fire, and vapour of smoke:
>
> The sun shall be turned into darkness, and the moon into blood, before that great and notable day of the Lord come:
>
> And it shall come to pass, that whosoever shall call on the name of the Lord shall be saved. (Acts 2:17, 19-21)

If anyone thinks it would have been exciting to be living in Pompeii at noon on August 24, A.D. 79, he has something even more exciting to look forward to when the Lord shall come to fulfill His prophecy made through Malachi saying:

> For, behold, the day cometh, that shall burn as an oven; and all the proud, yea, and all that do wickedly, shall be stubble: and the day that cometh shall burn them up, saith the Lord of hosts, that it shall leave them neither root nor branch. (Mal. 4:1)

John the Revelator gives us a preview of our own last days that makes the last days of Pompeii look like a Sunday School picnic. John says:

> And I beheld when he had opened the sixth seal, and, lo, there was a great earthquake; and the sun became black as sackcloth of hair, and the moon became as blood;
>
> And the stars of heaven fell unto the earth, even as a fig tree casteth her untimely figs, when she is shaken of a mighty wind.
>
> And the heaven departed as a scroll when it is rolled together; and every mountain and island were moved out of their places.
>
> And the kings of the earth, and the great men, and the rich men, and the chief captains, and the mighty men, and every bondman, and every free man, hid themselves in the dens and in the rocks of the mountains;
>
> And said to the mountains and rocks, Fall on us, and hide us from the face of him that sitteth on the throne, and from the wrath of the Lamb:
>
> For the great day of his wrath is come; and who shall be able to stand? (Rev. 6:12-17)

In the excavations of Pompeii, her people were found in different situations. Some were in the streets attempting to escape. Some were found in deep vaults where they had gone seeking security. But where do you think they found the Roman sentinel? They found him standing at the city gate where he had been placed by his captain. His hands were still grasping the arms which had been given him to protect Pompeii from any possible outside enemy. And there, while the heavens threatened him; there while the earth shook him; there while the lava stream rolled around him; there he stood at his post doing his duty; and there, after the centuries had passed away, he was found.

So let us stand to do our duty at the posts where our captain has placed us. And may God help us that, when the explosion comes, we will be ready.

14

Christopher Sly, the Tinker

William Shakespeare was not an original writer, primarily. It has been said that Shakespeare used more quotations and fewer quotation marks than any of the great writers. He drew from many sources, all of which he improved and polished. The story of *Christopher Sly, the Tinker*, with which he begins his play, *The Taming of the Shrew*, is of Oriental derivation. A similar story appeared in the *Arabian Nights* and in Italian literature.

Christopher Sly was a tinker. That is, he was an itinerant mender of kettles, pans, etc. The dictionary says that a tinker is a tramp, a vagrant, a wanderer. He may be a rascal or a rogue. The picture of this occupation is about as low as could be imagined.

Shakespeare's story begins with Christopher Sly in an ale-house. While he was drunk he did a lot of damage. Owners of the ale-house threatened to bring in the police, but that was of no consequence to Christopher Sly. He had nothing with which to make good the damage anyway.

While the owners were sorrowing over their misfortunes, Christopher Sly dropped into a deadly, drunken sleep. This not only posed the problem of what the owners should do about their broken bottles and glasses, it also raised the question of what they should do with Sly's inanimate body.

While they were trying to figure out an answer, a nobleman and some companions stopped at the ale-house on their way home from a hunt. Their interest was quickly centered upon Christopher Sly because they didn't know whether he was dead or alive. When it was discovered that he was still breathing, the nobleman said of him:

O monstrous beast! how like a swine he lies!
Grim death, how foul and loathsome is thine image!

This nobleman had a fancy for practical jokes, so he decided to work out a psychological experiment in human behavior with Christopher Sly as his subject. The nobleman said to his companions:

Sirs, I will practice on this drunken man.
What think you, if he were convey'd to bed,
Wrapp'd in sweet clothes, rings put upon his fingers,
A most delicious banquet by his bed,
And brave attendants near him when he wakes,
Would not the beggar then forget himself?

First Huntsman:

Believe me, lord, I think he cannot choose.

Second Huntsman:

It would seem strange unto him when he waked.
[He would soon adopt the condition of his better self.
His previous life would then be only as an unpleasant]
        dream or worthless fancy.

Nobleman:

Then take him up and manage well the jest:
Carry him gently to my fairest chamber
And hang it round with all my [finest] pictures:
Balm his foul head in warm distilled waters
And burn sweet wood to make the lodging sweet:
Procure me music ready when he wakes,
To make a dulcet and a heavenly sound;
And if he chance to speak, be ready straight
And with a low submissive reverence
Say 'What is it your honour will command?'
Let one attend him with a silver basin
Full of rose-water and bestrew'd with flowers;
Another bear the ewer, the third a [scented towel],
And say 'Will't please your lordship [to] cool your hands?'
Some one be ready with a costly suit,
And ask him what apparel he will wear;
Another tell him of his hounds and horse,
And that his lady mourns at his disease:
Persuade him that [for some years past] he hath been lunatic . . .
[But in reality] is nothing but a mighty lord.
This do and do it kindly, gentle sirs:

First Huntsman:

My lord, I warrant you we will play our part,
As he shall think by our true diligence
He is no less than what we say he is.

Nobleman:

Take him up gently and to bed with him;
And each one to his office when he wakes.

The nobleman then arranged to have a group of players enter-
tain Christopher Sly when he awakened.

Another participator in this experiment was a lady who played
the part of his wife. She acted in all respects like a great lady, and
bore herself with the honorable action she had observed other great
ladies do unto their lords. To the drunkard she was to speak with soft,
low tones and lowly courtesies and say:

'What is't your honour will command,
Wherein your lady and your humble wife
May show her duty and make known her love?'
And then with kind embracements, tempting kisses,
And with declining head into his bosom,
[Have her] shed tears, as being overjoy'd
To see her noble lord restored to health.
. . . See this dispatch'd with all the haste thou canst:

Scene two takes us into the elegant bedchamber of this wealthy
lord where we see the sobered Christopher Sly being attended to by
many servants who had been assigned to wait upon him with rich
clothing, delicious food, extravagant luxuries. The nobleman himself
was there to do him homage. Sly's first request upon awakening was
for another pot of ale.

The first servant said, "Will't please your lordship drink a cup
of sack?"

The second servant said, "Will't please your honour taste of these
conserves?"

The third servant said, "What raiment will your honour wear
to-day?"

Christopher, confused about what all of this meant, said:

I am Christopher Sly; call not me 'honour' nor 'lordship:'
I ne'er drank sack in my life; and if you give me conserves, give

me conserves of beef: ne'er ask me what raiment I'll wear; for I have
no more doublets than backs, no more stockings than legs, nor no more
shoes than feet; nay, sometime more feet than shoes, or such shoes
as my toes look through the overleather.

The Lord said to him:

Heaven cease this idle humour in your honour!
O, that a mighty man of such descent,
Of such possessions and so high esteem,
Should be infused with so foul a spirit!

Sly said:

What, would you make me mad? Am not I Christopher Sly, old
Sly's son of Burton-heath, by birth a pedlar, by education a card maker,
by transmutation a bear-herd, and now by present profession a tinker?
Ask Marian Hacket, the fat ale-wife of Wincot, if she know me not:
if she say I am not fourteen pence on the score for sheer ale, score
me up for the lyingest knave in Christendom.

But those participating in the charade didn't listen to Christopher
Sly. They began the process of persuading him that he was really a
great nobleman and that his memories of failures and miseries were
only bad dreams of that long mental illness which had now been cured.
Each contributed to the idea that his servants, friends, and his lady
had grieved and suffered during these years and had continually prayed
for his recovery. Then the lord said to him:

O noble lord, bethink thee of thy birth,
Call home thy ancient thoughts from banishment,
And banish hence these abject lowly dreams.
Look how thy servants do attend on thee,
Each in his office ready at thy beck.
Wilt thou have music? hark! Apollo plays,
And twenty caged nightingales do sing:
Or wilt thou sleep? [You shall have a scented couch.]
. . . Say thou wilt walk; we will bestrew the ground:
[Before thee with flowers,]
Or wilt thou ride? thy horses shall be trapp'd,
Their harness studded all with gold and pearl.

Dost thou love hawking? thou hast hawks will soar
Above the morning lark: or wilt thou hunt?
Thy hounds shall make the welkin answer them,
And fetch shrill echoes from the hollow earth.

First servant:

Say thou wilt course; thy greyhounds are as swift
As breathed stags, ay, fleeter than the roe.

Second servant:

Dost thou love pictures? we will fetch thee straight
Adonis painted by a running brook.

What impact do you think this made on the mind and will of
Christopher Sly? He had lived a life of poverty, rejection, drunkenness, and then—one day—he woke up in a magnificent room, in a
most comfortable bed, with clean sheets. He was told by many people that he was a nobleman of great wealth and power, that he had
just miraculously been restored from a sickness in which he had
imagined living the most wretched kind of life.

He saw evidences on every hand that substantiated what he was
being told. Present in the room were servants waiting to do his slight-
est bidding; seated at his bedside was his beautiful, devoted, adoring
wife, concerned only with his pleasure and welfare. All these evidences
could not possibly be disregarded. Think what an impact this might
have on you if you had been in the place of Christopher Sly.

But now Christopher had to make a decision. He said:

Am I a lord? and have I such a lady?
Or do I dream?

Then he gave his own answer when he said:

. . . I [have] dream'd till now?
I do not sleep: I see, I hear, I speak;
I smell sweet savours and I feel soft things:
Upon my life, I am a lord indeed,
And not a tinker nor Christopher Sly.

It is natural for anyone to believe those things he wants to believe
and which are told convincingly enough to him by enough people over
a long enough period. As the wise man Solomon said, "As he thinketh
in his heart, so is he" (Prov. 23:7).

We may remember the story of Bunker Bean who was tricked into success; but as long as he believed himself great, he was great. Many people have felt that they were born to greatness, then they wentto work to prove it to themselves so that their wildest, most unbelievable dreams have come true.

But this important process also works in the other direction. When Christopher Sly had thought little, sinful, irresponsible thoughts he not only became a tinker, but a drunken, irresponsible tinker as well. Upon first seeing Christopher, the nobleman had said of him, "O monstrous beast! how like a swine he lies! Grim death, how foul and loathsome is thine image."

The course of Christopher Sly lay along that broad, meandering road mentioned by Jesus that leads to death. Those who go that route not only lose faith in God, they also lose faith in themselves. The most widespread disease in the world may well be an inferiority complex. When we load ourselves up with guilt, drunkenness, and sin, we end up as tinkers, not only in this life but in the life to come.

Many people today are turning themselves into tinkers. There are young people who dress in the most ludicrous clothing, let their uncombed hair grow, take pride in their unwashed appearance. They delight in rebellion, immorality, and a kind of drug addiction that goes far beyond the worst that Shakespeare could figure up for Christopher Sly. If they continue, they will end up in a place where they do not want to go.

If these people really wanted to make themselves feel like noblemen, all they would need to do is follow the course pursued by the attendants of Christopher Sly. They could give themselves a hot soapy bath, have their hair cut, dispose of the soiled and smelly rags of the tinker. Then they could take pride in their personal appearance, dress themselves in the robes of noblemen, believe in themselves, develop qualities of greatness, righteousness, and responsibility to match their station.

It is probable that Shakespeare had several things in mind when he wrote this story of Christopher Sly. It was written partly for entertainment, but the entire story through it also carried the most magnificent lesson of uplift in that "as he thinketh in his heart, so is he."

We ought to remember that each one of us is a very important person. We are children of divinity, formed in God's image, endowed with His attributes and potentialities, heir to His glory. We

can convince ourselves of this all-important fact by surrounding ourselves with that faith and those virtues that cannot do other than exalt
us. Then we will have those joys that will make us glorious.

15

Year of the Locust

Some time ago, Fred J. Greve discussed an interesting philosophy concerning the important role human tragedy plays in life. Life is a mixture of pleasure and pain, ease and hardship, success and failure. Usually there is some relationship, or balance, between them.

There are many circumstances in every life over which we have little or no control. However, our attitude about our adversity, and what we do as a consequence of adversity, is often far more important than the event itself. Fortunately for us, we have full and complete authority over our own reactions.

Mr. Greve tells about a vast horde of locusts that visited certain parts of South Africa. As the locusts poured over the land, landowners rushed out to try to kill them or drive them away. But all efforts seemed useless. The land became barren. Waving fields that once gave a verdant expression of hope were stripped of their growing treasure. The tangible promise of future sustenance became, instead, devastation.

After the South African insects had gorged themselves, they died and were piled up in rows. Then these broken-hearted, impoverished people plowed the dead predators into the ground. From the fertilizing strength thus added to the soil by the bodies of these natural enemies came the best crops they'd ever had.

Throughout the rest of their lives, these people kept that year of tragedy alive in their memories. They referred to it as the "Year of the Locust."

Such experiences have plagued mankind ever since time began. Egypt had her seven years of famine. History is replete with wars and difficulties. The two once great nations of Israel and Judah were carried away to foreign slavery.

These instances remind us of the statement made by the ancient prophet Joel. He said:

> That which the palmerworm hath left hath the locust eaten; and that which the locust hath left hath the cankerworm eaten;

and that which the cankerworm hath left hath the caterpillar eaten. (Joel 1:4)

It is common for each of us to have personal periods of depression and much suffering. Yet our years of personal tragedy may also be remembered in this way: our heartbreak and trouble may also be followed by our most productive years. John Milton said: "No one ever does his best until he has suffered much."

The Lord spoke to a latter-day prophet about problems that were almost unendurable. He said: "Know thou, my son, that all these things shall give thee experience, and shall be for thy good" (D&C 122:7).

At another time, speaking of very severe difficulties, the Lord said: "If thou endure it well, God shall exalt thee on high" (D&C 121:8). So, frequently, it is not the problem itself but how we handle the problem that is important.

It is significant that our world was planned for good. This was indicated by the Apostle Paul when he said to the Romans: "All things work together for [the] good . . . [of] them that love God" (Rom. 8:28). That is, if we love God, if we think right, if we have the right attitude, then everything works for our good. Uphill is as important as downhill; labor is as necessary as ease. Disappointments can build our character quite as effectively as will pleasant surprises if we have the right attitude about them. Even crickets will leave us a benefit if we love God.

It requires hard pounding to make good steel; sometimes the best thing that can happen to us is to get a good swift kick in the pants. It is our enemies who keep us alert and on our toes, whereas the opiate of the over-kind friend often puts us to sleep and invites disaster. Opposition in our lives often does for us what a good sparring partner can do for a professional fighter. But a good fighter is required to pay an opponent to give him a good licking three times a week, whereas life often gives us a licking designed for our improvement and charges us nothing.

Many years ago I knew a young man who had a drunken, ne'er-do-well father, but this young man loved God. He thought straight. Nothing could have been a more potent teacher of righteousness than this close-up view of his father's bad example.

Even Satan is permitted upon this earth for our benefit. That is, God could destroy Satan at any instant He desired. "Then," we might ask, "why doesn't He?" He himself gave us the answer:

> And it must needs be that the devil should tempt the children of men, or they could not be agents unto themselves; for if they never should have bitter they could not know the sweet. (D&C 29:39)

We are the offspring of God; a little pounding on His anvil can often make our lives better.

Oscar Wilde once said that if God wished to punish us all He would need to do would be to answer our prayers. That is, if all our prayers were fully answered no one would ever get sick. No one would ever die. We would always get our own way. We would have no difficulty, and there would be no strength. Even sickness and death serve our eternal purposes as well as do health and life.

An important part of our existence is the fact that into each life some rain must fall. If all we knew was bright sunshine, our entire earth would be a vast Sahara Desert. However, life sends us no problems that we can't solve if we love God and have the right attitude about those problems.

It may be that the Lord had this in mind when He spoke to the prophet Joel:

> Be glad then, ye children of Zion, and rejoice in the Lord your God: for he hath given you the former rain moderately, and he will cause to come down for you . . . the former rain, and the latter rain . . .
>
> And the floors shall be full of wheat, and the fats shall overflow with wine and oil.
>
> And I will restore to you the years that the locust hath eaten, the cankerworm, and the caterpiller, and the palmerworm, my great army which I sent among you.
>
> And ye shall eat in plenty, and be satisfied, and praise the name of the Lord your God, that hath dealt wondrously with you: and my people shall never be ashamed. (Joel 2:23-26)

One of the challenges in our world of opposites is learning how to deal with our problems. Because the good and the evil grow side by side in God's world of free agency, we sometimes select the evil; or sometimes we look with envy at our erring friends and talk ourselves into adopting their sins by saying to ourselves, "Everybody's doing it."

You can't judge whether a thing is right by the number of people who are doing it—or not doing it. No righteous person could reasonably argue that to be drunken is good for us, or that immorality advances our best interests, or that lying helps us to be happy. Truth is not determined by what people may think about it.

An all-wise God determined what was right and what was wrong even before this earth was formed. He has said, "If ye love me, keep my commandments." But because we become arrogant and proud when the Lord sends us blessings, He is compelled to send the locust to bring us back to our senses. Only then can we get hold of the plow and make fertilizer for our land out of our problems. It is because of our unsolved problems that the scriptures foretell wars, pestilence, famine, and earthquakes that will desolate the earth in the last days.

Our present cold war, and the various hotter wars that presently eat up such a large part of our substance, are warnings to us because, by and large, we are not repenting of our evil, either nationally or individually. Even though we are having an increase in nervous disease, and even though our national debt is going up, we are not plowing under very many locusts to make the future years better.

Professor Greve told about those who did fertilize their lives with their problems. For instance, William Wilberforce was a small, sickly English preacher. For twenty years he did not have a moment without pain, even though he was often under heavy sedation. But Wilberforce used this pain to develop in himself sympathy for others.

Later James Boswell wrote of him, "When I went to hear him preach, I saw a shrimp in the pulpit. But as I watched and listened, he became a man of great stature before my eyes." The agony of Wilberforce helped him grow in wisdom. He so stirred up the conscience of England that she voluntarily freed her slaves.

Pearl S. Buck, the writer, grew up in a land literally devastated by the locust. Her parents were missionaries in China where Pearl was born and where her parents both lie buried. Serious tragedies came into this young girl's life. For one thing, her daughter was retarded.

But Pearl S. Buck plowed under her difficulties and so fertilized her life that she wrote many best-selling books. Her *Good Earth* won for her the Pulitzer Prize for literature. Of her "year of the locust" she wrote, "There is an alchemy in suffering—one that gives inner growth and restoration."

Nathaniel Hawthorne saw several years of the locust. He had twelve frustrating years of unemployment. Then he had a job at the Boston Customs House, but he lost that job two years later when the administration changed. He became a surveyor until another change of administration left him stranded again.

Just as he was achieving success as a writer, Hawthorne was struck by another terrible tragedy. He saw his beloved wife, her dress aflame, burn to death. He tried to beat out the flames with his hands but he couldn't. After her death, Hawthorne became lonesome and desolate. Nevertheless, he went on to translate Dante's *Divine Comedy* into English, and he did much creative literary work.

We try to avoid affliction, yet sometimes it can prove to be our salvation. It has triggered some of the world's greatest accomplishments. When the lessons are plowed into the inner person, new insights can be born. New response patterns and new capabilities may produce their most abundant crop in the shreds and shards of broken lives. If we have enough DDT to stop the locust on the outskirts of town, we should certainly learn our lesson and do it.

But if some should get through to start eating our wheat, we might wonder if the Lord isn't trying to get a message through to us. If we will fertilize our lives with the lesson, He will, as Joel says, send the former rains and the latter rains, and our floors shall be full of wheat, and our vats will overflow with wine and oil. Then the Lord will repair the damage done by the locust.

May God give us many good years; but may He also help us to make the most of our "year of the locust."

16

Cardinal Wolsey

One very interesting Shakespearean character is Cardinal Wolsey who makes his presentation to the world on the stage of Shakespeare's Henry VIII. Wolsey was a Cardinal who served under the direction of the Pope at Rome. Because of a disagreement between the Pope and King Henry, Catholics in England withdrew from the rule and support of the Pope when King Henry established the Church of England.

Wolsey, who cast his lot with King Henry, was one of the most powerful men of his day. He served Henry almost as his right arm. He was a man of great power and great influence, although he was often ruthless in handling his power as he dealt with those who came under his influence.

Wolsey had a great lust for power. He had ambition and good prospects, even to become the Pope of Rome. He had secret correspondence with Rome behind the King's back. In a mix-up in his correspondence, he sent the letter intended for the Pope to Henry by mistake, a letter he did not want Henry to read. Also, unintentionally included in the correspondence was a list of all the property Wolsey had accumulated for himself on the side while he was handling some of the affairs of England which had been assigned to him.

Wolsey was one of the judges when Henry divorced his first wife, Katharine. When the King discovered Wolsey's secret correspondence, when he learned that Wolsey became enormously enriched while he was supposedly in the service of his country, King Henry immediately released Wolsey from his position. In one of his great speeches, Wolsey revealed a broken heart.

The Cardinal had made and unmade Kings and kingdoms. But, along the way, he had done evil, thinking, as most of us do, that the end would not find him out. In his last hour he found himself discovered, discredited, and discarded. His property had been confiscated by the state, which Henry ruled. His robes had been withdrawn by

the Church of which Henry was the supreme head. In the humble
place where he went to die, Wolsey said,

[I have done not well, and may God have mercy on my soul.]
Farewell! a long farewell, to all my greatness!
This is the state of man: to-day he puts forth
The tender leaves of hopes; to-morrow blossoms,
And bears his blushing honours thick upon him;
The third day comes a frost, a killing frost,
. . . And then he falls, as I do
. . . Never to hope again.

Then he said,

. . . I have ventured,
This many summers in the sea of glory,
But far beyond my depth: my high-blown pride
At length broke under me, and now has left me,
Weary and old with service, to the mercy
Of a rude stream . . .

And then he said to his servant, the only one who had not forsaken him:

[Oh, Cromwell] Cromwell, I charge thee, fling away ambition:
By that sin fell the angels; how can man then,
[Created in] the image of his Maker, hope to win by it?
. . . O, how wretched
Is the poor man that hangs on princes' favours!

Then he said to Cromwell:

Corruption wins not more than honesty.
. . . Be just, and fear not.
Let all the ends thou aim'st at be thy country's,
Thy God's, and truth's; then if thou [diest]
. . . Thou [diest] a blessed martyr!
. . . O Cromwell, Cromwell!
Had I but served my God with half the zeal
I served my king, he would not in mine age
Have left me naked to mine enemies.

17

Mark Antony

The longer I live, the more excited I become about the many wonders of this earth on which we live. But, in spite of its laws, its wealth, its utility, its miracles of performance, the greatest wonder in the world is still people. One of the most important facts about people is that they have problems to be solved.

It may be interesting to recount the history of the world and follow the rise and fall of great nations. Man has a lust for power; he often tries to gain control over other people. There is an important passage of scripture which says:

> We have learned by sad experience that it is the nature and disposition of almost all men, as soon as they get a little authority, as they suppose, they will immediately begin to exercise unrighteous dominion. (D&C 121:39)

History indicates that man has gone to war with his neighboring tribe or overthrew some kingdom other than his own. Down through the ages man has made slaves of his fellowman. If there is no other enemy in the field, he often seeks to exercise unrighteous dominion over his wife or other family members.

Shakespeare's story of Julius Caesar is an interesting study of this fickleness that can be seen in the nature of human beings. Julius Caesar came to power by the overthrow of the mighty Pompey. And Shakespeare has his character, Marcellus, say of the people who were so quick to change their allegiance:

> You blocks, you stones, you worse than senseless things!
> O you hard hearts, you cruel men of Rome,
> Knew you not Pompey? Many a time and oft
> Have you climb'd up to walls and battlements,
> To towers and windows, yea, to chimney-tops,
> Your infants in your arms, and there have sat
> The live-long day with patient expectation

To see great Pompey pass the streets of Rome:
And when you saw his chariot but appear,
Have you not made an universal shout,
That Tiber trembled underneath her banks
To hear the replication of your sounds
Made in her concave shores?
And do you now put on your best attire?
And do you now cull out a holiday?
And do you now strew flowers in his way
That comes in triumph over Pompey's blood?
Be gone!
Run to your houses, fall upon your knees,
Pray to the gods to intermit the plague
That needs must light on this ingratitude.

But Caesar hadn't been in office very long before others were planning his overthrow. Ultimately a group of conspirators assembled by Cassius, under the direction of Brutus, all friends of Caesar, approached the throne under a friendly pretense and killed Caesar with thirty-eight dagger wounds when he was without protection and unable to defend himself.

Caesar's death opened the way for the conspirators to rule the Roman Empire as they planned; but even before they got underway, another enemy arose to overthrow them in the person of Mark Antony, a friend of Caesar. As Antony looked down on the bleeding carcass of his friend, he said:

O mighty Caesar! dost thou lie so low?
Are all thy conquests, glories, triumphs, spoils,
Shrunk to this little measure? Fare thee well.

Mark Antony said of Caesar:

His life was gentle, and the elements
So mix'd in him that Nature might stand up
And say to all the world "This was a man!"

After the death of Julius Caesar, the world was divided into two great war camps. One was led by the conspirators under Brutus. The other was led by Mark Antony and Octavius Caesar. A long, hard, destructive war followed.

During this period, Mark Antony distinguished himself as one of the greatest generals who ever lived. He took upon himself the hardest tasks. He lived for weeks on a diet of insects and the bark of trees. He won the unquestioned loyalty of his men, the acclaim of the people, and the support of Octavius.

Opposed by such dedication and strength, the enemy generals one by one began to drop out of the fight. Finally Mark Antony stood where Julius Caesar once stood: master of the world.

It might be worthwhile to try to determine how he did it.

Someone gave a partial explanation when he said of Mark Antony: Armed with his convincing speech, the power of his logic, the courage of his leadership, and his own self-discipline, he swept everything before him. But when the need for effort was past, Mark Antony became idle. (Another lesson we might learn from this is that the worst mistake anyone can make in his life would be to become idle.)

Mark Antony went to Egypt, and there he fell in love with the bewitching Queen Cleopatra. He became a victim of the soft luxury, perfumed elegance, and immorality of the Egyptian court. His great mind became clouded by the fumes of wine. Shakespeare says, "In him we see the triple pillar of the world transformed into a strumpet's fool." At another time, Shakespeare called Mark Antony a "fishing rod general."

As he allowed his personality to disintegrate, Antony lost the loyalty of his men, the acclaim of the people, and the support of Octavius. Finally, a guard of Roman soldiers was sent from headquarters to take Antony into custody and take him back to Rome in chains. To take Mark Antony did not require an army now—just a few ordinary soldiers.

Mark Antony avoided arrest by thrusting a dagger into his own heart. As he lay dying, he told Cleopatra that there had been no power in the world sufficient to overthrow him except his own power. He said, "Only Antony could conquer Antony."

Contemplating the arrival of the Roman soldiers, Antony made his last speech about himself to Cleopatra which William Haynes Little has translated into verse.

Let not Caesar's servile minions
Mock the lion thus laid low.
'Twas no foe man's arm that felled him,
'Twas his own hand struck the blow.

He who pillowed on thy bosom
Turned aside from Glory's way,
When made drunk with thy caresses
Madly threw a world away.

One of the functions of great literature is that in so many cases, as is true with Mark Antony, we can see success and failure, good and bad, contrasted in the same life. Our opportunity is to make the most and the best of the good. We should always remember, "Only Antony can conquer Antony."

18

How Readest Thou?

Writing is fundamental to the preservation of our histories, our cultures, and our faith. But there is another blade associated with this writing "scissors" which has equal importance; that is reading. Writing is the means by which we identify and preserve greatness, but reading is the process by which this greatness is transferred to us and made usable in our own minds and hearts.

There are several kinds of reading. We skip-read to find specific items we need. We fast-read to get masses of information on our mental radar screen where it can be sorted and used later. Then there is a reading for pleasure.

We remember the occasion in Luke when the lawyer stood up tempting Jesus:

> Master, what shall I do to inherit eternal life?
> He said unto him, What is written in the law? how readest thou?
> And he answering said, Thou shalt love the Lord thy God with all thy heart, and with all thy soul, and with all thy strength, and with all thy mind; and thy neighbour as thyself.
> And he said unto him, Thou hast answered right: this do, and thou shalt live.
> But he, willing to justify himself, said unto Jesus, And who is my neighbour?
> And Jesus answering said, A certain man went down from Jerusalem to Jericho, and fell among thieves, which stripped him of his raiment, and wounded him, and departed, leaving him half dead.
> And by chance there came down a certain priest that way: and when he saw him, he passed by on the other side.
> And likewise a Levite, when he was at the place, came and looked on him, and passed by on the other side.

But a certain Samaritan, as he journeyed, came where he was: and when he saw him, he had compassion on him,

And went to him, and bound up his wounds, pouring in oil and wine, and set him on his own beast, and brought him to an inn, and took care of him.

And on the morrow when he departed, he took out two pence, and gave them to the host, and said unto him, Take care of him; and whatsoever thou spendest more, when I come again, I will repay thee.

Which now of these three, thinkest thou, was neighbour unto him that fell among the thieves?

And he said, He that shewed mercy on him. Then said Jesus unto him, Go, and do thou likewise. (Luke 10:25-37)

We assume that this lawyer was a highly educated man. He knew all the answers except the most important one: that any man who needed help was his neighbor.

The question asked by Jesus "How readest thou? . . ." might be connected very closely to the one Philip asked of the Ethiopian eunuch. An angel of the Lord had directed Philip to leave the place where he was and go toward the south. On his journey, Philip came upon an Ethiopian eunuch who had much authority under Candace, Queen of the Ethiopians. This man had charge of all the Queen's treasures.

As Philip approached, the eunuch was sitting in his chariot reading from the scripture the words of the prophet Esaias. Philip approached this man and said:

Understandest thou what thou readest?

And he said, How can I, except some man should guide me? (Acts 8:30-31)

Philip told the Ethiopian that he thought he could help, so the Ethiopian invited him to sit with him in his chariot to help him understand the scriptures. Under Philip's skillful tuterage, the eunuch not only understood: he believed. As they rode on they came to a body of water. The eunuch asked Philip to baptize him.

And Philip said, If thou believest with all thine heart, thou mayest. And he answered and said, I believe that Jesus Christ is the Son of God. (Acts 8:37)

How important these two questions are! Number one: "How readest thou?" Number two: "Understandest thou what thou readest?" The Bible is one of our most important resources, yet it does not do us any good as long as its doctrines and convictions remain in the Bible but never get into us, either in our understanding or in our actual living.

Surveys have shown that most people do very little constructive reading after their formal education is ended. This would mean that, because of the evaporation constantly taking place in our memories, information stored in our minds during our school years may become largely lost.

It is thought that one of the most important skills we can acquire is to learn to read effectively. The following suggestions may help us to help ourselves.

1. We should remember that mere reading does not compare in its value with a good reading habit. A good reading habit can place us among the educated and successful ones of our day in a very short time and, at the same time, make the process pleasant as well as profitable.

2. We should plow deep enough in our reading that ideas uncovered become our permanent property. Sometimes we allow ideas to skate so lightly above the surface of our brains that they do not remain long in our possession. We should develop a reading ability so that we know what the author said and meant, what we think about it, and what we are going to do about it.

3. By reading effectively we can actually learn to get out of a book more than there is in it. To be able to do this is a valuable skill. In some ways, reading a book is like any other process of invention or discovery. We add to it as we think about it and use it, and we ought to take notes as we read.

4. We ought to learn to correctly pronounce the words we read and use. We ought to know what they mean. We ought to think about applications of those words and how we can use the ideas they present.

5. Some people are "eye-minded": sight is the most important entrance to the mind. Other people are "ear-minded." A soldier gets his orders through his ears and, consequently, the orders increase in importance in his understanding. Some people develop a still greater ability to understand by utilizing the double focus of eyes and ears.

They read aloud to themselves so that the impulse comes not only by sight but also by sound.

When we learn to read, we ought to develop the ability to read to ourselves convincingly and entertainingly and with as much harmony and music as possible. We don't like to listen to a boring, dull, unenthusiastic reader or speaker who makes the most exciting ideas unpleasant. But we can put ourselves to sleep, intellectually, quicker than anyone else can. When we are bored with our own performance, the needle of our brain does not record very much.

6. In more ways than one, we ought to learn to follow the Ethiopian eunuch in developing a great interest in and sincere love for righteousness. One passage of scripture says that Cain loved Satan more than God. We are in trouble when we love cheap, profane, and vulgar ideas more than we love high-mindedness and intellectual power.

7. One of the most beautiful reading aids is memorization. We like best those personal friends we have known and loved for a long time. And our love usually increases as we get to know these friends better.

We enjoy singing best the beautiful music that is most familiar to us. We love magnificent pictures that become a part of us. As we learn to love people, so also can we form an affinity for important ideas, memorable experiences, and great biographies in literature. Those ideas that are stamped more permanently into our hearts by memorization are the ideas that can most readily and advantageously change our lives.

Great literature is not on trial. The reader is the one who is on trial. Our world has recorded the greatest ideas of the finest minds, including the ideas of God Himself. But what we do about it will largely depend on our learning to read and our establishment of good reading habits.

We must learn to read, to read understandingly, to read effectively, to read continuously, to read the finest things, and do the most worthy deeds.

19

The Mountain of Miseries

Many years ago Joseph Addison wrote an interesting parable under the title *The Mountain of Miseries.* He had been pondering in his mind the celebrated thought of Socrates that if all of the misfortunes of mankind were cast into a common stock and then redistributed equally to everyone, those who formerly thought themselves the most unfortunate would be much more contented than if they traded problems with any other person.

Mr. Addison says that, as he was turning this idea over in his mind, he fell asleep and dreamed that Jupiter issued a proclamation that every mortal should bring his griefs and calamities to a great plain appointed for that purpose and throw them into a common pile.

In his dream, Mr. Addison was stationed in the center of the plain where he could observe everything that took place. His heart melted as, one by one, he saw the whole human species marching by, groaning and moaning under their burden of griefs and miseries. Then in obedience to the decree, and with great joy, they threw down their various loads of care in the appointed place.

The pile grew quickly into a prodigious mountain. One man threw down his poverty, another his ill health, another his unsavory reputation. There was a multitude of old people who, with great delight, threw down their wrinkles and aches and pains. Many put down disabling worries, haunting fears, and distracting guilt complexes.

A most interesting part of this procedure, Mr. Addison observed, was that many of the problems disposed of by this vast throng were more imaginary than real. Some threw down occupations they despised, some got rid of an incompatible spouse, a dominating parent, or a disobedient child.

Mr. Addison was surprised to learn that the largest part of this growing mountain was made up of bodily deformities. In the pile were heaps of red noses, large lips, rusty teeth, crooked backs, protruding stomachs, glass eyes, and wooden legs. But he was even more astonished by the fact that there was not a single vice or folly thrown into the heap. He had assumed that everyone would take this opportunity to get rid of his sins, his prejudices, or his various moral frailties.

One profligate fellow came loaded down with his crimes, but upon searching his bundle it was found that instead of throwing away his guilt, he had merely laid down his memory. Another worthless rogue flung away his conscience but hung onto his ignorance.

There was another peculiar thing about this ordeal: When the sufferers were free from their own burdens, they surveyed the heap of miseries left by others with great interest. When they discovered what items had been discarded by others, they could not understand why the owners had looked upon these things as burdens at all. Each sufferer regarded his own miseries as immense and almost insufferable, though he usually felt that the problems of others were so much smaller in comparison that they were fairly insignificant.

While this confusion of miseries and chaos of calamities was taking place, Jupiter issued a second proclamation in which he ordered that each person should pick up an exchange affliction and return to his habitation. A poor galley slave who had thrown down his chains replaced them with a case of the gout. Some exchanged their sickness for poverty. Some traded their hunger for a lack of appetite. Some traded care for pain, some traded pain for care.

Women in the group were engaged among themselves bartering for figures and features. One exchanged her gray hair for a carbuncle; another took over a short waist for a pair of round shoulders; a third traded in a homely face for a bad reputation. But, strangely enough, as soon as the blemishes were in the possession of their new owners, somehow they also became unsatisfactory. The sufferers now seemed to think that their new misfortunes and calamities were even more disagreeable than the old ones had been.

Then Mr. Addison described the pitiful conditions that existed when the items of misery were laid upon the backs of the wrong people. The whole plain was now filled with many groans and heavy lamentations as these sufferers wandered around under the severe pain of their new and more intense pressures.

Finally, Jupiter took compassion upon the poor mortals and ordered them a second time to lay down their loads. Each was then to take back his own miseries. But Jupiter did more than that; he also sent the Goddess Patience to preside over the redistribution. As soon as the sufferers had accepted the philosophy of Patience, the size and disagreeableness of the mountain of miseries sank to a mere fraction of its former importance.

As those involved developed appreciation for the suffering of others, they lessened the amount of brooding they were inclined to do over their own difficulties. The wounds in their own hearts were partially healed by the discovery that every life was tormented by a sorrow that was more painful than their own.

Henry Wadsworth Longfellow wrote an exquisite poem in which he described the sweet relief that always comes to our own hearts when we share in the suffering of someone else. He said:

And I thought how many thousands
Of care-encumbered men,
Each bearing his burden of sorrow
Have crossed the bridge since then.

The particular evils that befall us are usually suited and proportioned to our own strength and need. Any evil often becomes more supportable as we become accustomed to bearing it. It is also frequently true that our problems and defects are actually blessings in disguise.

There is an old legend to the effect that the apostle Paul was a hunchback, and that he may also have been afflicted with epilepsy. Paul described his situation by saying,

And lest I should be exalted above measure through the abundance of the revelations, there was given to me a thorn in the flesh, the messenger of Satan to buffet me . . .

For this thing I besought the Lord thrice, that it might depart from me.

And he said unto me, My grace is sufficient for thee: for my strength is made perfect in weakness . . .

Then, in recognizing his affliction as his blessing in disguise, Paul continued:

. . . Most gladly therefore will I rather glory in my infirmities, that the power of Christ may rest upon me. (2 Cor. 12:7-9)

Now, as then, the world is filled with infirmities. Paul had his thorn in his flesh. Demosthenes had his speech impediment. John

Milton was blind. Beethoven was deaf. Lincoln was unhappily married. Each suffered with his own problem, yet to each his own affliction was the best.

However, in addition to those blessings that are sent to us in disguise, we usually take upon ourselves some unnecessary burdens we were never intended to suffer. We carry with us many difficulties that we should immediately get rid of. These are the problems we bring upon ourselves.

Many valuable moral points were mentioned in Mr. Addison's vision that can help us secure an advantage for ourselves in carrying our burdens:

First, we should never repine about our own misfortune.

Second, in comparing our neighbor's suffering with our own, we should not add too much from our imagination.

Third, if we regard the sorrows of others with sentiments of humanity and compassion, our own burden will be lightened.

Fourth, this vision calls our attention to the dangerous inclination some of us have to drop our troubles while clinging for dear life to the vices that cause them.

Fifth, Paul referred to some faults of the Corinthians and said, "For this cause many are weak and sickly among you, and many sleep" (1 Cor. 11:30). We often destroy our own health and dig our own graves when we improperly lay unnecessary griefs upon our souls.

When Jesus said, "Bear ye one another's burdens," He may have had in mind that an appreciation for the cares of others, and a desire to help them, may be the best way to lighten our own load.

But Jesus went far beyond Mr. Addison. Even before the world began, God formulated a program, not merely for exchanging our miseries or even of learning to bear them more agreeably. He provided a Savior to take our entire load of miseries upon Himself and leave us free and clear of our problems. It was only a thorn-crowned, bleeding Christ that could pay the penalty of our sins and win the salvation and adoration of the world.

One of the most beneficial ideas, and one of the most magnificent thoughts in the universe, is this great program of divine atonement. The Son of God was appointed to take upon Himself the sins of all men upon the condition of their repentance, and without any need for them to bear the miseries of anybody else in exchange.

As we repent, our problems are dropped into a pile of sin, misery, and error that will be borne by the Redeemer of all mankind. As a part of our worship, we sing a sacred hymn.

> How gentle God's commands,
> How kind his precepts are.
> Come cast your burdens on the Lord
> And trust his constant care.
>
> Beneath his watchful eye
> His saints securely dwell.
> That hand which bears all nature up
> Shall guard his children well.
>
> Why should this anxious load
> Press down your weary mind?
> Haste to your Heavenly Father's throne
> And sweet refreshment find.
>
> His goodness stands approved
> Unchanged from day to day.
> I'll drop my burdens at His feet
> And bear a song away.

What a tremendous idea! And what a magnificent opportunity these words represent!

It is a stimulating experience to stand in the pulpit on the Sabbath day and look into the faces of a congregation of fine, intelligent, faithful people. They are dressed in their best clothes; they have come to the house of prayer to worship God, to better inform themselves, to have their spirits quickened. In some particular virtue, life expects all of us to excel everyone else.

Ralph Waldo Emerson said that he had never met anyone who was not his superior in some particular. This applies to every child of God. Believing this, the one standing in the pulpit might well think that everyone present was inwardly calm and completely free from care in every form. But a closer investigation may reveal that, behind every face, there lurks some problem involving a load of fear and misery.

Many Christian churches send ushers down the aisles every Sunday to collect the contributions of those present. Wouldn't it be a wonderful idea if we could send ushers down our aisles to collect our sins and miseries.

However, the ushers would need containers much bigger than those required to hold the people's contributions. Some very large baskets would be needed. When they were filled, their weight would be much greater than any usher or set of ushers could carry.

But all of this great load of difficulty can be dissolved in our lives by the atonement of Christ. If we live our lives righteously, we may soon feel the release from our sins. Then what a thrill we might have to stand up and joyously sing, *Praise God From Whom All Blessings Flow.*

The gospel of Jesus Christ is like a great mountain of joys from which we may select the most worthwhile satisfactions. But isn't it strange that instead of picking up virtues, we seem more anxious to pick up the bad habits and evil deeds of other people? Then, for the balance of our lifetimes, we struggle under the resulting oppressive weight of misery.

How much better it would be to throw these burdens down, as the Lord desires us to do, and to pick up the joys of obedience, the satisfactions of faith, the thrills of righteousness so that we can bear away the virtues of a noble character, a love of truth, and the promise of eternal glory.

20

The Great Stone Face

Nathaniel Hawthorne was a great author. He loved people, and he kept in close touch with life. One of his constructive philosophies was indicated in his story of the *Great Stone Face*.

High up on a cliff in the White Mountains of central New Hampshire, formed in an arrangement in the rocks, was what appeared to be a great stone face. For ages this stone image looked down upon a spacious valley where many people built their homes and cultivated the rich soil on the gentle slopes and level surfaces of the valley.

Obviously the great stone face was a work of nature; but some people felt that its majestic dignity exercised a kind of divine guardianship over the valley below. They felt that, by the kindness of its natural expression, the great stone face was intended to be the teacher of the people. The aspirations it expressed enlarged their hearts and filled them with wider and deeper sympathy. And who could tell but what the spirit of this valley had sculptured its own likeness into the magnificent human image that reigned upon the mountain top.

This great stone face, which stood a hundred feet high, bore the broad arch of the forehead, the nose with its long bridge, and the vast lips which, if they could have spoken, may have proclaimed their philosophies of life from one end of the valley to the other. It seemed positively to be alive; it seemed to have more than a human interest in the people and what went on in the valley below.

With the great stone face before their eyes, it was a happy place for children to grow to manhood and womanhood. Because of the truth of the old proverb that says we become what we admire, it was an education merely to look at the great stone face. According to the belief of many people, the valley owed much of its fertility and prosperity to this benign influence that continually watched over it, purifying the atmosphere and infusing its vitality into the sunshine.

One afternoon when the sun was going down, a mother and her young son sat at the door of their cottage talking about the great stone face. They had but to lift their eyes and there it was, plainly to be seen with the sunshine brightening its features. While the gigantic visage smiled down upon him, Ernest said, "Mother, I wish that it could speak, for it looks so very kindly that its voice must needs be pleasant. If I were to see a man with such a face, I should love him dearly."

The mother answered, "If an old prophecy should come to pass, we may sometime see a man with exactly such a face as that."

"What prophecy do you mean, dear mother?" asked Ernest. "Pray tell me all about it."

So his mother told him the story that her own mother had told to her. Her account was not of things that had passed but of what was yet to come. It was a story, nevertheless, so very old that even the Indians who formerly inhabited the valley had heard it from their forefathers. And their forefathers had heard it murmured by the mountain stream and whispered by the wind among the treetops.

The prophecy was that, at some future day, a child should be born in this valley who was destined to become the greatest and noblest personage of his time and whose countenance, in manhood, should bear an exact resemblance to the great stone face.

Ernest, clapping his hands above his head, cried, "Oh mother, dear mother, I do hope I shall live to see him."

His mother was an affectionate and thoughtful woman. She said, "Ernest, perhaps you will."

Ernest never forgot the story his mother had told him. It was always in his mind. He spent his childhood in the cottage where he was born. He was dutiful to his mother; he grew up to be a fine man under her expert tutelage and that of the great stone face. When the toil of the day was over, he would gaze upward until he imagined that those vast features personally recognized him and gave him a smile of encouragement responsive to his own look of veneration.

It may have been that the great stone face looked more kindly to Ernest than to any other, that the boy's tender, confiding simplicity probably discerned what other people could not see. As he built up these great loves and attitudes within himself, he began to teach them to others as they met each evening beneath the trees.

Several times a rumor spread among the people that someone looking like the great stone face had been seen among them, but the illusion never lasted very long. The discouraged people would go back to wait for another.

With each disappointment, Ernest would say, "This is not the man of the prophecy, and so we must wait longer yet."

As he looked up to the image, Ernest seemed to sense that a smile beamed over his whole countenance with a brightening radiance. The great stone face seemed to him like a magnificent guardian angel seated among the hills enrobed in a vesture of gold and purple.

This visual grandeur was accentuated by the western sunshine as it melted through thinly diffused vapors that had swept between Ernest and the image he gazed at so confidently. But as it always did, the countenance of his marvelous friend gave him courage and hope. It seemed to say, "Fear not, Ernest, he will come."

More years sped swiftly and tranquilly away. Ernest still dwelled in his native valley as a man of middle age. By imperceptible degrees he had become favorably known among the people. Now, as heretofore, he labored for his bread, he was the same simple-hearted man that he had always been. He had thought and felt much; he had given away many of the best hours of his life trying to do good for his fellow men. It sometimes seemed as though he had been conversing with the angels and had absorbed some of their wisdom unawares.

Almost involuntarily Ernest became a community teacher. The pure and high simplicity of his thought, which was one of the manifestations of his great stone friend, took shape in good deeds dropped silently from his hand. His audience never suspected that Ernest, their own neighbor and familiar friend, was much more than an ordinary man. Least of all did Ernest, himself, suspect it.

The saddest of all Ernest's disappointments came when he beheld a man who might have fulfilled the prophecy but did not will to do so. Each time Ernest turned again to the great stone face to see the majestic grandeur it had worn for untold centuries, the benign lips seemed to say, "Lo, here I am, Ernest. I have waited longer than you and am not yet weary. Fear not, the man will come." Years hurried onward, treading in their haste on one another's heels.

College professors, even the governing men of cities, came from far and near to converse with Ernest. The report had gone abroad that this simple man had ideas unlike those of other men. They had not been gained from books but were of a higher tone. Whether it were sage, statesmen, or philanthropists, Ernest received these visitors with the gentle sincerity that had characterized him from boyhood. He spoke freely with them of whatever was uppermost in their minds or lay deepest in their hearts.

While they talked together, Ernest's face would kindle, unaware, and shine upon his guests as with a mild evening light. Pensive with the fullness of such discourse, they took their leave and went their way. Passing up the valley, they would pause to look at the great stone face, thinking they had seen its likeness in a human countenance but could not remember where.

Songs of a great poet found their way into Ernest's hands. He read them after his customary toil. Seated on the bench before the cottage door where he had long filled his repose with thought by gazing at the great stone face, he now read those exciting stanzas that caused his soul to thrill within him. He lifted his eyes to the vast countenance beaming on him so happily.

"Oh majestic friend," he murmured, addressing the great stone face, "is this poet not worthy to resemble thee?" The great stone face seemed to smile but answered not a word. Then the poet came to see Ernest. About his arrival, Ernest said, "Methinks I never saw the great stone face look so hospitably upon a stranger."

The poet sat with Ernest. They talked together. Often had the poet intercoursed with the wittiest and wisest, but never before with a man like Ernest whose thoughts and feelings gushed up with such a natural freedom. He made great truths familiar with his simple utterance. Ernest was moved by the living images that came from the poet's mind and peopled the air around the cottage door with shapes of beauty. The sympathies of these two men raised them to a height that neither could have attained alone.

As Ernest listened to the poet, he imagined that the great stone face was bending forward to listen also. Then, as had been his custom, Ernest went at evening to discourse to an assemblage of neighbors in the open air. Ernest and the poet went arm in arm, talking together as they went.

Then Ernest began to speak, giving to the people what was in his mind and heart. His words had power because they accorded with his thoughts; and his thoughts had reality and depth because they harmonized with the truths he had always practiced. The poet, as he listened, felt that the being and character of Ernest produced a nobler strain of poetry than he had ever written.

Then, high up in the golden light of the setting sun, appeared the great stone face with a white mist around it like the mantle covering Ernest's brow. Its look of grand magnificence seemed to make the world a better place. At that moment, in sympathy with the thought he was about to utter, Ernest's face assumed a grandeur of expression so imbued with benevolence that the poet, by an irresistible impulse, threw his arms aloft and shouted, "Behold, behold, Ernest is himself the likeness of the great stone face." Then all the people looked and saw that what the deep-sighted poet said was true. The prophecy was fulfilled!

This account of Nathaniel Hawthorne is much more than merely an interesting story. It represents a great philosophy of life—that we become the embodiment of our own ideals which can then be communicated to others. We can also embody the ideals of others for the benefit of all.

In 1925 the great sculptor, Gutzon Borglum, gave us another "great stone face" story. He carved into the granite face of Mount Rushmore, in the Black Hills of South Dakota, in figures four hundred sixty-five-feet high, the images of George Washington, Thomas Jefferson, Abraham Lincoln, and Theodore Roosevelt. Each year over two million people visit Mount Rushmore and look up into the stone faces of these four great American ideals.

As the life of Ernest was lifted up by the great stone face, even so others have been made better by knowing the great character qualities of these Black Hills presidents. Everyone enshrines in his own heart the image of some great benefactor to have that ennobling power over him. More than almost anything else in the world we need heroes we can look up to, and admire, and reverence.

Somebody has said that the holy scriptures is a great collection of God's *Who's Who*. The scriptures contain the ideals and ambitions of those heroes who are important to God. With the word of the Lord upon their lips, they look down over the valley of our earth to contribute their greatness to our lives.

Then, above all, we have the countenance and direction of the Redeemer of men Himself, who gave divine instructions and who gives continual inspiration by which we may qualify for His living eternal presence. Jesus Himself said, "And this is life eternal, that they might know thee the only true God, and Jesus Christ, whom thou has sent" (John 17:3).